The Playful and Powerful
WARRIOR
YOU!
within

*How to reclaim your personal power and live
a fulfilling life of true adventure.*

GJ REYNOLDS

Published by Beachlifestyle Publishing, LLC

For more information, contact Beachlifestyle Publishing at:
www.BeachlifestylePublishing.com

Beachlifestyle Publishing, LLC
8635 West Sahara Avenue, #578
Las Vegas, Nevada 89117
www.beachlifestylepublishing.com
simplyg@beachlifestylepublishing.com
www.powerfulwarrior.com

To order additional copies, contact order@beachlifestylepublishing.com

Cover and interior design: JENNINGS DESIGN/www.jenningsdesignonline.com

ISBN-13: 978-0-9832295-0-6

LCCN: 2010919235

First Edition 2011

Printed in the United States of America.

10 9 8 7 6 5 4 3 2 1

I dedicate this book to the following:

*My parents, Gary and Nancy;
my grandparents, Mimi and Papa, and Nana and Pop;
and my children, Rachel, Michael, Marcus, and Austin.*

I continue to learn many lessons from all of you.

I thank you all.

CONTENTS

FOREWORD

■ ■ ■

Life can be so difficult at times that it is easy to become frustrated, disillusioned, bewildered, unhappy, and depressed. GJ Reynolds has come to the rescue with his sincere, thought-provoking plan to find success and happiness in a mixed-up world. His transparency about his own depression and thoughts of suicide gives his words credibility.

The deeper you get into this book the more vividly you will see a clear view of who you are, how to reclaim your powers, and how to lighten up the load of negativity that might be leading to your anxiety. GJ's words will give you the incentive to discover the true purpose of your life.

If this fine book gets the proper advertising, marketing, and promotion, it would be no surprise to me to see it on the list of best sellers.

DALE BROWN
Former LSU Basketball and Hall of Fame Coach
www.coachdalebrown.com

PREFACE

■ ■ ■

Come, be open and embrace your magnificence. Play through any fears and reclaim your personal power. No experience necessary.

■ ■ ■

Why did I write this book? I wrote this book because first, the grace of God showed me how I could transform my life and the lives of others. Second, most of the people I come in contact with are searching for some type of transformation in their very own lives, and what has worked for me may very well work for them. Third, the steps laid out in this book are what have transformed my life as a Playful and Powerful Warrior, and I have chosen to share them with the world.

In 1972, I met Coach Dale Brown, former LSU basketball coach, National Coach of the Year, and Hall of Fame coach. I was just eleven years old. Throughout my life, he shared many philosophies on basketball as well as on life. All of his teachings have had a major impact on the man I am today. He has been a coach, teacher, and mentor. Most importantly, he is one of my closest friends. Because of his mentorship and friendship, many of the principles he has taught me are in this book. Just like Coach, I have chosen to share my knowledge and experiences.

In November 1973, Coach Dale Brown invited coaches John Wooden and Adolph Rupp to the LSU Purple and Gold kickoff game. I had the distinct pleasure of meeting John Wooden, former UCLA basketball coach (named the Greatest Coach of the 20th Century by ESPN) as well as mentor and friend of Coach Brown; Hall of Fame coach Adolph Rupp, the former basketball coach at Kentucky; and Bob Pettit, the two-time All-American at LSU, who was later inducted into the NBA Hall of Fame.

At that game, Coach Wooden patted me on the head and said, "You look like a fine young man. Just practice the fundamentals and you will go far." Coach Rupp patted me on the head as well and said, "Just do what he [Coach Wooden] said and you will do just fine." Bob Petit then said, "Young man, what they said is the best advice I can give you. Just do what they said." Thanks to all three of you, I realize that when my life is balanced and in order, I am practicing the fundamentals of life.

After meeting Coach Wooden in 1973, I was introduced to him again in 2007 by Coach Brown. Then, in 2008, I had the distinct pleasure of fulfilling one of my most desired goals: to spend an afternoon with Coach Wooden.

I have read and listened to everything Coach Wooden has written and taught. This piece he wrote stays with me: "Everything in the world is passed down. Every piece of knowledge is something that has been shared by someone else. If you understand it as I do, mentoring becomes your true legacy. It is the greatest inheritance you can give to others. It is why you get up every day: to teach and be taught."

Thank you, Coach, for sharing. It has become my passion and my purpose to help millions of people transform their lives. Consequently, this is a primary reason I have written this book: to assist others in reclaiming their personal power and be the playful and powerful Warriors they are. Most are closer to having all of their goals, dreams, and aspirations than they realize. They just require a little assistance and the willingness to do so.

I wrote this book to be used as a beginning tool with the potential to evoke lasting life changes in anyone who reads it. I choose to teach the reader how to embrace his or her inner playful and powerful Warrior self and live a fulfilling life of true Warrior adventure.

Need a little help?

I was the guy who had a great amount of agony and pure anguish prior to writing anything. The internal anguish was so great that I never wanted to write anything. Now I choose to write. I have also learned to love to write.

About fifteen years ago, I told John McNaught, my business partner at the time, "If you could just get paid to write all day, you would be right at home and the happiest man I know." What I meant by that statement was that John loved to write and had written many great documents. He was always at peace when writing anything.

I was just the opposite. I was good at adding my input to what he wrote. That was about it.

What changed? Today, I consider myself a student, teacher, and coach. A student who loves to learn. A teacher who loves to share information and teach others. A coach who loves to assist others to have and achieve their desires with purpose. I simply draw from my own life experiences, education, and lessons. Writing is one of the ways for me to gather my thoughts and choose to share them with others.

The more I share with others, the more I find it empowering. I find it a keen sense of fulfillment. So now I write. I find writing peaceful and relaxing. I have now found that same peace about writing I would always see within John. I find it amusing that I am now a writer and author.

Others have considered me to be focused, intense, direct, strong, and powerful. Only my closest friends, family, and associates ever saw my playful side. Everyone saw my powerful side. I was typically the one who would lead, especially when things were tough. I outwardly portrayed my inner strength. It was a false strength, my ego. I learned that true power comes from the inside for strength and flow. I will cover more of this throughout the book.

Coach Dale Brown shared with me three key things when I was younger:

1. Always try to do your best.
2. Never give up.
3. Let God take care of the rest.

These three simple teachings have helped me transform into the man I am today. They assisted in saving my life when I was suffering from depression and was suicidal. These teachings have also become a catalyst for this book.

In May 2007, I was with Coach Dale Brown in Lawrence, Kansas. We were walking outside of Allen Field House (where the University of Kansas Jayhawks play basketball) and Coach asked me, "When you came out of depression and from being suicidal, outside of God, what was the major thing that made an impact on you?" I replied, "Coach, just getting around the right people." From that moment, I started adding to Coach's teachings this statement: "Get around the right people."

I have always been a consistent goal setter, and I have encouraged people always to have "Big, big goals, dreams, and aspirations." I have said on many occasions, "If you are going to shoot for something, shoot for something big. You just might receive it." I added "Big, big goals, dreams, and aspirations" to Coach's teachings and started teaching this as well.

During this time, I was seeking how to live and enjoy my true, authentic self. This led to me sharing "Be authentic; live authentically."

From there, I was also learning how to accept and enjoy living in "the now." I had always done a great job of living in the future. I was great at putting off enjoying "the now" for the enjoyment I thought I would have later. I was great at living a life with delayed gratification. I realized I am able to live right here and right now.

Since I am able to live only right now, I have started to be conscious of being and living in the moment. I have started to see a new and empowering life for myself and have begun sharing "Live in the now" as well.

> **When you open yourself to the development of your inner Warrior self, concrete change is destined to occur.**
>
> ■ ■ ■

Then, one weekend in the spring of 2008, I went to a "Warrior" weekend. One of the exercises was to listen to the instructor describe a beautiful and tranquil setting. He described a young and happy boy playing. Then he said, "You are this young boy. He is playing with a ball and the ball bounces over to an animal. What animal is it? What do you see? What do you feel?"

For me, it was a playful and powerful tiger. The tiger was interacting with me, and together we were having fun. I felt the security of the tiger, and I felt the strength and power of the tiger, too. I was at peace, and I could feel the love I had with the tiger. Tranquility illuminated within me, and it was a loving and magnificent feeling.

Then the instructor said, "You are both: the boy and the tiger. You are one and you are the same." I realized right then and there that I am a playful and powerful tiger. I *am* a playful and powerful Warrior.

Hence, this is how the title of this book came to be. What I will teach you here is all about reclaiming the playful and powerful Warrior within YOU. It is finding, maintaining, and living with your loving, tranquil, peaceful, playful, powerful, and magnificent self.

This book is a direct result of the following:

- Having great teachers, coaches, and mentors.
- Having experienced some fun, some challenging, and some very difficult times.
- Having Coach Brown ask me one simple question.

I trust each one of you who reads this book will find something useful, and then apply it and pay it forward. Now go and *embrace YOUR playful and powerful Warrior within YOU!*

Be playful, be powerful, and live your life to the fullest.

■ ■ ■

CHAPTER ONE

■ ■ ■

Your Warrior Journey

Are you ready to live your great Warrior journey?

■ ■ ■

Imagine it is the middle of June. The day is warm and sunny. It's peaceful and calm. A slight breeze is blowing. The trees are blooming.

A man walks out on his back deck to view all of this beauty. The sun shines on his face and he feels the warmth. The birds chirp a lovely melody, and two squirrels play tag in the trees. He has a nice cup of coffee, and the taste is refreshing. He smells the freshness in the air.

There is no one around. Just the man. He is alone and one with nature. It seems as though there is a magnificent feeling in all of this—pure tranquility, beauty, and peace. Everything is green, and everything is alive.

All of a sudden, all he sees is darkness. All he feels is emptiness. All he hears is chatter. All he tastes is blandness. All he smells is death. He is depressed and numb to the world.

Death is imminent.

Right now, all he is thinking about is ending it here and now. He is tired of feeling like a failure, of struggling to pay his bills, of being fearful of losing everything, and he is ashamed at how he has let so many people down and is unable to meet his basic obligations.

This is a forty-year-old man who is a college graduate, former sergeant in the US Army, corporate executive, leader of thousands, successful entrepreneur, and overall high achiever who is now a broken man. He is at his lowest point in life, and all he desires is for all of this negativity and depression to end and go away. He is looking for the light at the end of the tunnel and is unable to see it.

The guilt. The shame. The emptiness. Seems too much to bear.

The only apparent answer is to end it all, with the use of a Ruger 9 mm. To die by his own hand.

All of a sudden, a brightness illuminates around him. An easy peaceful feeling fills him up. The numbness disappears. He sees a bright haze. Then, just as he would grab hold of a child to get his or her attention, he is grabbed and held in this same stern and loving way.

A distinguished voice says, "You do not have a reason to die. You have a reason to live. I will show you how."

> ## You have a reason to live.
> ■ ■ ■

A calming effect comes over him, and he feels completely filled with love inside of him. He looks out at the beauty of the world with amazement. He wonders what just happened. He looks to see whether anyone else is around. There is only him.

He asks himself what just happened, if this was all a dream. His consciousness is aware he is alive and that all of this was—and is—real. There is both a sense of confusion and a sense of understanding within him. The thoughts of never giving up and always doing his best comes into his consciousness. Then . . . everything goes blank.

He finds himself at the bottom of a shower with the water running. He begins to weep. The more he weeps, the more he feels a cleansing. The tears pour out of him and onto the bottom of the shower. Again, everything goes blank.

The next day he wakes up in a fog. Was all of this a dream? He realizes this is *his* life and *his* reality. The events from the previous day begin to come into focus.

He asks himself, "How could I have reached this point? Who was the stern and loving being? What did this stern voice mean by 'I will show you how?' How to do what? Was this God reaching out to me?"

He gets through the day, still feeling confused and shameful. He finally goes to bed, and the bed feels like a sanctuary. Warm, comfortable, safe, and secure. His eyes close.

He falls into a deep sleep. He is in the midst of a dream. A dynamic and vivid dream that is much more than a vivid dream. It is a vision. Every step and every moment, he feels more alive and empowered.

Suddenly he sees this dynamic Warrior. He looks around. He notices thousands of people watching the Warrior and listening to him share his story.

He follows and watches this Warrior speak all across the country and the world. At every stop, he witnesses this Warrior share his story with millions of people worldwide. He witnesses the impact of this Warrior and feels connected to him.

Every moment he is present, and he wonders who the Warrior is. He is dynamic, interesting, playful, and powerful. The audiences are captivated with every word of this Warrior's story. The man feels the impact and witnesses the cleansing and empowerment that is happening with each stop along the journey of this Warrior.

At one particular venue, there are 13,189 people present. The Warrior walks out onto the stage and begins to share his story. The same story he has witnessed all over the world.

With each word, the man becomes aware that the Warrior's story is similar to *his* story. Then the realization hits. This *is* his story. A bright light begins to shine on his face, as if he is on a stage with all of the lights shining on him.

He feels the sweat start to appear on his forehead and on the side of his face. He opens his eyes and looks out at the crowd. They are all waiting to hear him speak. He feels the energy of the crowd. He feels completely at peace, whole, and alive.

And then he realizes he *is* the Warrior. The same Warrior speaking to millions of people around the world, sharing *his* story. What story? It is *his* personal Warrior story, the one that tells all of his life's journeys, trials, tribulations, and adventures.

He wakes up the next day. Everything is just as it was before he went to sleep. The bills are unpaid. The shame is present. And so too are the same depressed feelings that had him on the brink of committing suicide.

Just the man and God know what has transpired and how he feels. There is a new, refreshing feeling in him. In his soul, he knows something good will come from all of this.

He is also open to understanding what this is all about. He chooses to learn what adjustments are necessary for him. He understands he has a life to live, and *he has chosen to live it.* He knows his journey, and his great adventure is one he chooses to explore.

This is *his* life. Some of you may be able to identify with this story because it is similar to *your* story or to the story of someone you know and care for.

Personally, I am able to relate closely to this man. That magnificent day was June 19, 2001. How do I know this? This is *my* story. This was the start of my new beginning to my current Warrior journey and adventure.

> **Your story has power.**
> **Share it with others.**
>
> ■ ■ ■

Regardless of where you currently are in your life, you have a life to live—your powerful Warrior adventure and journey. All you have to do is *choose* to live it.

Congratulations on making it to this very moment. After all, this is your life. Tell your story. One of the most powerful things you are able to do is share your story. Love it, live it, and share it. Are you open and ready to live and be the best that you are? Are you living your great adventure? Your present situation merely determines where you start.

I look back at how I got to this very point. Through all the ups and downs, it has been a great adventure. What I am personally excited about is that the most exciting part of my life's journey starts today. Every day is a new day for me, and my journey is still in process. Every area addressed in this book is one in which I am still improving.

Do you feel inside yourself a higher purpose calling for greatness within you? Do you choose to live your great adventure? You are able to do, have, or be whatever you choose. You are able to experience being more alert, aware, and present. All you have to do is choose the necessary time investment for yourself. Time is a precious gift. How will you choose to use the time you have?

> ## Do you feel inside yourself a higher purpose calling for greatness within you?
>
> ### ■ ■ ■

Remember the joy of childhood? Think about it. Virtually everyone experienced some type of freedom, exquisite happiness, and absolute calm at some point in childhood.

When I was growing up, most of us were childhood Warriors. We were taught to pray to God and allow Him to guide us. We looked to Him and the stars above. We were authentic in what we said and did. We were taught to do our best and, in most cases, we did. Forgiving our friends was much easier when we were kids, and once we did, we moved forward as if nothing had ever upset us. We simply let go and moved on. We had loving and caring teachers, neighbors, friends, and family surrounding us.

We dreamed big, big goals, dreams, and aspirations. We used our imaginations. We knew what we desired to be when we grew up. For me, it was Batman.

I was also taught to go after what I chose to have out of life. My attention span was limited to what was going on right then and there. I was living in the present moment. Life was all about living and having fun right then and there.

With the assistance of like-minded Warriors—and by looking within yourself—you are able to live the life you deserve to have and dreamed about as a child. It is time to start *living your* life. Do you realize you have the power to see, think, and choose differently for yourself? Being open to seeing things and doing things differently will change your life.

At some point in your life, you will reach a crossroad. Are you at your crossroad right now? It may be a crossroad in finding peace, happiness, life, health, prosperity, balance, success, children, marriage, or a new career. You determine whether you have and live a better lifestyle path and establish a more fulfilling life. Many events and experiences may seem to be too difficult and create tremendous hurt, fear, and paralysis.

Have you ever been certain you were on the right path, only to find out the path you were on seemed to lead to an offramp or a dead end? Too often we find ourselves at a different point than where we choose to be. Your Warrior journey is likely to have all sorts of exits, detours, circles, and perceived dead ends. Remember, it is simply a journey. Please embrace it and choose to enjoy the process. You have the POWER to choose again. Step up and into your own empowering adventure.

This book serves as a jump-start to being in touch with your inner self. You are able to choose to embrace *your* Playful and Powerful Warrior self. For some of you, it is reigniting your synergy or reaching a much greater height. This book will assist you in finding your authentic path and staying on *your* path.

Many people are seeking freedom and independence from the social chaos of the external world. They often find the path less traveled is the one that leads to personal empowerment and freedom. Your internal Warrior self will help you find your *authentic path* and shape *your* vision of how you choose to live and be. It will most likely be the road you have avoided choosing so far.

Your path is paved with dreams of a better life and a more secure future. You determine your own path. You control your perception of *your* world and you control *your* thoughts, words, and actions.

Your success is dependent on your own internal realization, effort, energy, and desire. Your life has magnificent possibilities. Experience the difference of owning and living your life while having fun doing so. Start a new path for yourself today by reading, learning, and choosing the best choices and actions for you.

Once you have decided to choose the path to your personal freedom and look for a way to achieve your goals, dreams, and aspirations, the path becomes clearer. Your path leads to the clearing where you will have a clear view of your life—who you are and the goals, dreams, and aspirations you seek. The intangibles are now tangible; the vision is clearer. You are now on the threshold of embracing your powerful self and life. Once you cross over and into the clearing, everything you imagined will be achievable. The amazing thing about this is that you will end up with the life you choose.

Understanding the Warrior within you may at first seem a little foreign in your present world. Warriors correct certain things within themselves before they begin to succeed and come into their own magnificence. Warriors are willing and able to overcome, in a positive manner, any obstacles or challenges they may face. As a Warrior, you will encounter many life experiences in your journey.

When your playful and powerful Warrior self is embraced, you are able to see a manifestation of what God has planned for you. You are an empowering Warrior entrusted with all the keys to your kingdom.

Are you willing to release the imprisoned Warrior from the dungeon you have placed him in? Understanding your previous behavioral thoughts, words, choices, challenges, and actions will enable you to do so. You have the power to allow your authentic Warrior self to be free.

**YOU have the POWER
to CHOOSE again!**

■ ■ ■

> # Your present situation merely determines where you start.
>
> ■ ■ ■

Your success is as predictable as the sun rising in the east and setting in the west. Practicing and implementing the Warrior lessons and principles in this book, you will move to the front of the line in life. Your life.

When you consistently and persistently apply these lessons and principles, you live life from your true, authentic self and have all of the success you deserve. You are the architect of your path. You are behind the steering wheel of your life, and you control the pace at which you live it.

You have gifts, talents, and abilities far greater than anything you have ever realized or used up to now. You have within you the potential to accomplish wonderful things with your life.

I trust that you will restart your life's journey as well. You have the power to choose the necessary adjustments for yourself. You are able to live your life, from this day forward, as a great adventure.

When you come from your true, authentic self, your life becomes much more enjoyable to live. You are a magnificent human being and you are . . . a Warrior. Be playful, be powerful, and embrace your Warrior journey.

Are you committed to your Warrior journey and living your great adventure?

■ ■ ■

WARRIOR ACTION STEPS

■ ■ ■

YOUR WARRIOR JOURNEY

**Your Warrior journey is endless
and will go on to the very last
moment of your warrior life.**

1. Choose a moment and congratulate yourself for making it to this very moment.

2. Commit to living your Warrior journey.

3. Are you feeling there are more things for you to accomplish in life? Create a list of what they are.

4. List three adventurous things you choose to accomplish.

5. List three things you choose to change in your life starting right now.

6. Your story is unique and is powerful. Share it. Purchase a journal and start writing your story.

■ ■ ■

**Be Bold, Be Playful, Be Powerful, and
Enjoy Your Great Warrior Adventure!**

CHAPTER TWO

■ ■ ■

Be Authentic;
Live Authentically

**When you honor yourself and
live according to your values, you
live your life with purpose.**

■ ■ ■

I had a great authentic childhood. As I became an adult, I
started to make subtle decisions and choices. I chose to honor
everything outside of my true, authentic self. Over time, bit by
bit, I seemed to get off course of my true authentic compass.
I began to disregard some of my feelings. I began to choose to
bury them. I became resentful and angry. I began to choose
decisions that made me act differently than honoring my true,
authentic self. I chose to honor everyone else's boundaries. I
placed my boundaries to the side.

At times I knew I was choosing compromising decisions and cross-
ing the boundaries that were best for me. I would either justify
these decisions or create my own reasons for doing what I did to get
ahead in life. Over time, it started to have a toll on me.

Then one day I realized I was selling out. I was selling out for
others. I was selling out to achieve more. I was selling out for

11

the external world. I was selling out for what worked best for me. I was selling myself short of my own magnificence.

I share this with you because I was chasing and living an illusion. I was chasing after things and living externally—chasing, competing, and conquering my perception of the "American Dream."

Many times in my adult life, I was living what most would call the "American Dream." I thought having money, multiple homes, multiple cars, and material things would provide me happiness. I found it satisfying that I could set goals and achieve them. It was refreshing to accomplish all of this. I found that I welcomed the compliments I received for achieving all this. All ego!

I began to chase having more, as if it were a drug. Why? I chose to have more than one car, one home, one watch, one more this and one more that. I became an addict of chasing and having more stuff. I had to have more than just one of something. I had to have the latest and greatest.

Many of my friends and associates would comment on how great it would be to be me. They were happy for me in my successes. They recognized the accomplishments I had achieved and the challenges I had overcome.

One evening at home, I came to realize I was actually extremely unhappy. I was unhappy with my external world, and I began to look at how unhappy I was within.

While others saw greatness and accomplishment, I saw a sell-out. While others saw success, I saw failure. Externally I looked great. Internally I was a feeling like a complete mess.

I began to wonder how I could have so much externally and be so empty inside. At this point in my life, I had spent the better part of my adulthood chasing the external world and ignoring *living* in *my* internal world.

Then I started to seek out how I was able to live within my truest, most authentic self. I started to listen to my internal voice. I realized then that I was choosing to live my life being less than the best that I am. I had a thirst and hunger to also find out how to be the best that I am and live within my own truth.

I learned what worked best for me and to seek the boundaries that best suited me. I started understanding what truly worked for me in my life and using it for creating my own happiness. The more I looked within, the louder my inner voice and spirit started to speak to me. They began to tell me what was best for me. More importantly, I listened, and I started choosing the right course of action for me.

> ## Reclaim the authentic inner child in you.
>
> ■ ■ ■

Over time, I began to release my resentments, my hurts, and my anger. I began to allow my feelings to be open and alive. I began to forgive others. I began to forgive myself. I became more aware. I started to truly *live* again.

It was a rebirth of who I am, my authentic self. Each and every day, I am faced with the choices of honoring my true, authentic self. The more I have focused upon honoring myself, the easier it has been for me to choose what is best for me and to hear and listen to my inner self. I found what works for me, and now I honor it.

Are you asking yourself if there is an alternative or a different way to live or be? Being authentic requires the courage to face your personal truth. When you are authentic, you are being true to your innermost self. When you go on your authentic journey, you begin to leave behind the tension of being who you think other people want you to be.

This leads to knowing who you are and being true to it. It releases positive energy and enables you to achieve the deepest goals, dreams, aspirations, and ambitions that may have been suppressed from childhood. Authentic transformation focuses your energy on what you choose to have and to avoid areas of unwanted compromise in your life.

Living authentically, in its simplest terms, is living in your truth. Warriors understand and honor this truth. Living authentically brings out your truth in your heart, soul, and your authentic center. It allows you to be guided by divine truth and wisdom each and every day. It is living your greatest and most authentic life in the world. It is joyfully creating and living your highest purpose.

You are living an authentic life when you fashion a life where the decisions and actions you create are deliberate and in harmony with what is important for you. Focus on what is honoring you.

What is honoring yourself? It is simply doing what you know *is* best for yourself. You feel it in your gut, you feel it in your spirit, and you know that what you are choosing for yourself is what *is* best for you.

Others may choose to disapprove with your choices or offer suggestions about what is right for you. However, it is your life to live, and it is a life that you know in your soul is right for you. It is a life that causes you to welcome each day with passion, enthusiasm, and excitement.

Your original conditioning will help you be authentic. So how do you be authentic? You reclaim that child in you. Remember when you woke up as a child, happy with anticipation for the day? Remember the joy you experienced in having your friends over? Remember your parents' mixed reaction, when you blurted out some delightfully honest, blunt truth? Remember how you knew exactly what you wanted to be when you grew up?

Being authentic simply means being genuine. It means being the true author of your life. It means adhering to your own code of morals and values. It also means staying clear of the drama, chaos, and stress of others. It means being original, being complete, and honoring yourself. It is simply being *you*.

As you grow, you naturally question authority or the status quo. You have curiosity and the desire to understand how the world works. At some critical point, it is driven home to you that for you to get along in the world, you must sometimes withhold your opinions, listen to your elders, deny what you see and hear, lie low, or even lie. Each of us is born into a family or a situation that already has a code and a belief system that works to some degree.

You are told what you are unable to do or cannot do versus what you are able to do. You are molded by the external world, telling you how you should behave, look, or have. You begin the process of placing a lot of your feelings, beliefs, opinions, self-criticisms, pain, fear, disappointments, humiliations, anger, lack of acceptance, and feelings of distrust and abandonment in your very own closet. You have the idea that maybe it will all go away or you will sort it out later. Unfortunately, as all of this begins to pile up, you tend to lose your shining magnificence. Your bright light begins to dim. You begin to get off course and start to lose your true, authentic self.

No one prepared you for this. You were told that if you kept your head down and worked hard, you would enjoy the fruits of your labor. Having worked hard and having lived with the pressures from others and life in general, the questions remain: How am I able to live such a life? What steps am I able to choose toward simply being me? What is my life's purpose? What am I actually meant to be doing? How am I able to maintain my lifestyle and find happiness? The answer lies in your own personal authentic transformation.

In the early stages of life, you are often focused on pleasing others—parents, friends, associates, teachers, bosses, and spouses. In an effort to get your needs met, you learn to play by other people's rules. As you mature, you become more competent, independent, and able to meet your perceived needs. You are then less motivated to do what others want you to do. In many cases, you are tired of keeping up appearances and care much less about what other people think. Then you choose to live your own goals, dreams, and aspirations.

In short, you come to grips with the idea of being your own person and living as such. Now you choose to live a life that *feels* right. You choose to be free of inner turmoil and outer chaos. Instead of approval, you are more likely to seek a sense of inner peace, the kind that accompanies authentic living.

To be authentic, you must live in and with integrity. Warriors must first be clear about what is important to them, their internal codes. Simply put, someone who lives in integrity honors his or her personal values, actions, and choices, and aligns with his or her internal code. Everything inside is whole and undivided; he or she is complete.

Warriors understand what integrity is. They honor it and live it. It is ingrained in their systems. It flows with honesty. And it must be present in the spoken words that reflect their inner world. Warriors know when to say "yes" and when to say "no." It is that adherence to principles—both moral and ethical—that builds character and allows one to be a vibrant and authentic Warrior.

> ## Who decides whether you live a life of authenticity? You do.
>
> ■ ■ ■

> **Living authentically, in its simplest terms, is living in your truth.**
>
> ■　■　■

Integrity is about honoring your internal system. Most people prefer the truth. Is this true for you? The sooner the truth is available, the more quickly everyone will adjust accordingly.

At times, acting upon your integrity may seem uncomfortable in the moment, and doing so will quickly be followed by relief. It is freeing to say "no" to certain people, things, and events. Align yourself to what works for you. In your relationships, speaking a "hard truth" makes room for greater understanding and for deeper friendships to emerge. Living with integrity speeds up the process of realizing the potential and authenticity of your relationships.

Integrity is one of the great catalysts in life. Cultivating your own internal awareness about your values is the first step in expanding the integrity in your life. Knowing when to say "yes" and when to say "no" is a process of discovery that evolves throughout your life. Awareness allows you to identify your personal internal blueprint that will guide your decisions. Your willingness, courage, and discipline become the keys to living with this internal code and integrating it into your life.

Integrity is an internal guidance system that directs you along the path of your life. Freedom and energy arise when integrity is present. The more you honor it through your actions, the more fulfilling your life will be and the more quickly you will realize your goals, dreams, and aspirations.

Living within your truth allows you to live soulfully. Soulful living is about conscious living from the inside out to achieve deep happiness and fulfillment and to feel passionate about your work, life, relationships, and self. Soulful living allows you to use your talents to contribute something of real meaning in your world. Living authentically is the most important aspect of living soulfully.

> ## Soulful living is conscious living from the inside out.
>
> ■ ■ ■

When you are following your soul's wisdom, living your truth, and being real in every sense, you are living an authentic life. You are contributing your soulful nature and God-given talents and gifts to the world, thus creating a happier, more authentic, and more soulful life experience for yourself and for everyone around you.

How happy are you? Happiness seems to be elusive for many people. They often search for it in all the wrong places. I sure did. You may be seeking happiness in the instant gratification of your desires; in the accumulation of possessions, accolades, or relationships; in your accomplishments; or in the delights of your physical senses. The pursuit of happiness motivates many of your actions and efforts in life. You may be spending a great deal of time, effort, and money in the acquisition of "things," believing that once you have the right partner, house, car, bank balance, physical attributes, possessions, or children, you will be satisfied and fulfilled. You think happiness will descend upon you and remain your constant companion.

Most people desire to be happy and avoid suffering as much as possible. Many of them have found that it is suffering that leads to compassion, wisdom, and understanding. It is often your suffering that enables you to realize that happiness is derived from your internal self. I personally learned this when I was in the depths of depression and contemplating suicide. The outer circumstances of your life are simply a mask. Happiness is derived from within by being connected to your inner self and feelings.

Choose to connect to your feelings. Many of us have been taught judgment or value thinking, and we have learned to distrust or disconnect from our feelings. We have been desensitized, taught to endure pain without complaint, and told that it is an honor to sacrifice our mental state for society. As a result, many of us suffer from isolation and are prone to addictions and to acting out our feelings in dysfunctional ways.

Many people are afraid of intimacy. They hide behind masks that are brittle and in need of repair. They are sad, lonely, frightened, hurt, angry, and ashamed. With the loss of their feelings, they also lose what is most precious to them: their ability to honor themselves, to hold life dear, and to live authentically.

Some people know their feelings perhaps too well. They have learned to indulge in their feelings and use them to manipulate others, often the ones they love most. They lack the ability to stand in their own authenticity. They simply use manipulation to get what they desire, and they mask their true feelings and authenticity. Lost in their feelings, they also lose what is most precious to them: their ability to have trust and love authentically.

There is another way you are able to rediscover your feelings and true, authentic self. When you clarify what you are feeling and learn to express those feelings directly and authentically, you begin to learn to balance the depth of your soul with the wisdom of your mind.

Being authentic requires the courage to face your personal truth. Choosing your actions based on your internal awareness and applying that awareness to what is best suited for you will allow you to experience true harmony.

When you are birthing a more authentic version of yourself, you are *unconsciously* growing away from the familiar unspoken contracts and agreements you have with people and the external world. Being unauthentic, you experience some or all of the feelings or situations listed below.

Living within an *Unauthentic* Self

- You are skilled and successful in your career and are unhappy doing it.

- You are unsure of what you want for you. You are unaware that you are able to choose to live your life differently.

- You want close relationships; however, you escape to work, food, sex, drugs, alcohol, or something else instead of developing your own esteem and emotional aptitude.

- You know what changes would make your life more meaningful and still find excuses for not making and choosing the changes right now.

- You are being dishonest or untruthful with yourself or others.

- You are pessimistic.

- You have constant anxious feelings.

- You are noncommittal.

- You look to impress others.

- You are a people pleaser.

- You second-guess most decisions.

- You rationalize and defend most everything.

- You allow others to make your choices.

- You are rigid.

- You are nonnegotiable.

- You say or do things you regret.

- You have false or unrealistic expectations.

- You make constant judgments of others.

- You hide, bury, or deny your feelings.

- You have a victim consciousness mindset.

- You are paralyzed, stuck, or hyperactive.

- You seek, use, or have an addictive behavior.

- You feel confused and overwhelmed.

- You are irresponsible.
- You feel helpless or hopeless.
- You use manipulation, deceit, and mind games to get what you want.
- You are depressed.
- You feel resentment, hurt, and anger.
- You get trapped in endless mind chatter.
- You have constant negative internal chatter.
- You feel constant fear and vulnerability.
- You are unwilling to get or receive help.

> **The most valued and respected quality you are able to develop is a reputation for absolute integrity.**
>
> ■ ■ ■

If any of the above statements resonate with you, give some thought to what would bring your inner and outer worlds into finer alignment. Choose to be filled by being honest with yourself and with others about who you are. This will start to create a life that is right for you. At times, exploring and excavating your truth may seem like a daunting task. With all the busyness of your everyday life, self-reflection may seem self-indulgent. You may say to yourself, "I don't have time to sit around contemplating my life. I have got things to do, places to go, and responsibilities to meet."

This is the irony. By moving as fast as you are able to down a path that leads you away from your true self, you end up backtracking or going around in circles. You continue searching for *the* place that feels like home. When you choose to defer the time to tune in to what is best for you, you actually waste more time with many false starts and journeys that might otherwise have been avoided.

An authentic life is built from the inside out with attention to one's inner wisdom. Perhaps you could simply begin each day with a question: "What is important to me today?"

Once you are clear about what resonates with you, and you align your outer behavior with inner truth, your life will flow in a direction that is meaningful. You will gain energy from insight, evolution, and expression. When your inner and outer worlds are congruent, the pieces will all seem to fit, and everything will click.

When you know at your core that you are living a life that is aligned with your purpose, filled with what you love, and supportive of your growth, you are living an authentic life. Your outer behavior is fueled by your inner truth.

What you do reflects what you believe, how you feel, what you know, and, most importantly, how you live. When you live authentically, you know what you stand for and choose conscious choices to honor those values. Your highest priorities consistently get the lion's share of your time, and your actions are consistent with your beliefs. If fitness, family, prayer and meditation, and service are important to you, choose the time for them in your life. On the other hand, when you live in a way that feels uneasy, you might be concealing or ignoring parts of yourself that long to be acknowledged.

> ## You know what works for you and is best for you. Honor it.
>
> ■ ■ ■

Have you ever listened to your voice of your authentic self? This quiet and persistent voice whispers truth in peaceful moments—while you are driving down the road, in the middle of the night, when you are on vacation, or after you meditate or pray. Many call it intuition or a gut feeling. Intuition speaks in short, clear messages that are different from the repetitive mind chatter that makes you feel anxious. Intuition tells you where the authentic choice is for you. Your authentic choice for you will enhance your life and add joy to your life. See if the following statements ring true for you.

Living within Your *Authentic* Self

- You are skilled and successful in your career and are doing what you love.
- You know what you choose to have, and you do know it is the life you have and are living.
- You have open and honest close relationships.
- You know what changes would make your life more meaningful, and you choose action.
- You are honest or truthful with yourself and others.
- You are optimistic.
- You are flexible.
- You honor your commitments.
- You seek to please yourself.
- You are accepting.
- You are loving and compassionate.
- You are positive and open.
- You think for yourself.
- You are able to go with the flow.
- You are open to change.
- You choose to do your best.
- You know when to forgive—and do it.
- You know how to accept and receive love.
- You listen to your feelings.
- You choose responsibility for yourself with your choices, thoughts, words, and actions.
- You choose healthy choices for yourself.
- You know when to stop, reevaluate, and choose again.

- You know how to ask for help and are willing to do so.
- You realize only you are able to choose to be happy.
- You are tuned into a larger field of awareness.
- You accept and are open to your own vulnerability.
- You honor what works for you.

By focusing on many of the choices and statements above, and by constantly looking for ways to improve yourself, you will continually grow. This is how you find meaning in what you are doing and how you are living.

Choose to be somewhere you are able to reflect on what kind of person you have become and what kind of person you aspire to be. Choose one day a month and retreat to nature for an hour or so. Choose the time on a regular basis for self-reflection. Tune in to who you are, what you desire, and what is best for you next. The rest will unfold. Find yourself and be in touch with your inner self. Choose time each day to write some of your thoughts, activities, and desires in your journal. As you proceed, this will open many personal insights for you.

An authentic transformation is sustainable when you subject all areas of your life to evaluation and development. It means looking at the inner you, the way you live your life, your relationships, and your interaction with the external world. It means facing your fears about a leap toward what you desire and choose to have. Whatever it is, consider the time and effort as a worthwhile investment.

The return on your investment will be to live authentically as you choose. Make the authentic choice for you. Choose what works for you, honor it, and be authentic. Be the Playful and Powerful Warrior you are.

What adjustments are you able to choose to embrace your authentic self?

■ ■ ■

WARRIOR ACTION STEPS

■ ■ ■

BE AUTHENTIC;
LIVE AUTHENTICALLY

Is it my soul coming out in the open, or the ego of the world knocking at my heart for its entrance? —RABINDRANATH TAGORE

1. Living authentically, in its simplest terms, is *living in your truth.* List three things you are doing to live within your truth.

2. Look inward for your fulfillment. List three things you are doing for yourself to be whole and happy.

3. What are you currently doing to honor yourself? List three things you are currently doing to honor yourself.

4. Find the root of any discomfort you are experiencing. List three things you are currently experiencing any discomfort with, and then find the root causes and let go of them.

5. Increase the awareness of your integrity system. Choose action when you have a clear yes and when you have a clear no. Notice the impact on your life when you acknowledge your boundaries, and honor them. List three things you are able to say "no" to.

■ ■ ■

Be Bold, Be Playful, Be Powerful, and Enjoy Your Great Warrior Adventure!

CHAPTER THREE

■ ■ ■

The Playful and Powerful Warrior

A playful and powerful Warrior honors himself and the world around him.

■ ■ ■

We all have a playful and powerful Warrior inside. Finding and embracing your inner Warrior self will require some effort on your part. When you embrace your Warrior life, it will create a whole new perspective.

Imagine how you feel when you are being playful. As you step out of childhood and mature into adulthood, playfulness typically becomes a foreign concept. You are able to reclaim it and incorporate it back into your everyday life.

As I shared in the preface, all of my closest friends and associates noticed my playful and fun side. I periodically allowed my playful side to be seen by them. The more playful, light, and fun I was with them, the more playful, light, and fun they were. We were simply mirroring each other. Over time, I learned I was more productive when I accepted and embraced my playful side. When I was easygoing, my business teams and associates had more fun and were more productive, too. More importantly, in these moments, I was at peace with myself.

So how are you able to bring out your more playful side? Playfulness describes you when you are being fun, jocular, frisky, and creating amusement. Engage in activities that allow you to reclaim your childhood merriment, to embrace your light-hearted, silly, and fun side. You will find that your playfulness creates positive energy and smiles for you and those around you.

Playfulness brings out the fun in everyone. In a world where stress and anxiety is commonplace, a little playfulness is a perfect solution. Playfulness adds a new dimension, whether you are in a business meeting, with friends, or working on a creative project. How many business meetings have you participated in that were way too serious and could have used some playfulness?

Imagine yourself playfully engaging in conversation with others or playfully singing along to music. Imagine being playful with children. Imagine playfulness with your family, friends, coworkers, and associates. How do they all respond when you are playful?

Adopt it for yourself and see what you experience. Have fun, and let your playful Warrior side out for all to see. Choose to be lighter and less serious with yourself. Accepting your playful side is actually inner power being released. Playfulness is powerful.

> **Playfulness creates positive energy and smiles.**
>
> ■ ■ ■

Today's Warriors are full of fun and have high spirits. They are typically lighthearted and supportive. They enjoy humor and have fun in what they do. Warriors are expressing pleasure and amusement in their mission. They know showing their playful side brings out their inner strength.

In the past, I definitely showed some of my playful and fun self. On most occasions, I chose to ignore my lighter side. Why? Because I thought showing my playful side was a distraction and a weakness in my business and life. I thought I had to keep my fun side locked up and reveal it only when things were outside of business or serious matters. I would also show my playful side when all of my responsibilities were taken care of. I chose to wait and to delay letting out my fun authentic side.

I was keeping my playful side bottled up, and I became rigid and way too serious. That is when my friends and business associates shared their thoughts with me: "Your rigid side, the hammer and the hardness you sometimes display, creates stress for us. We all enjoy your playful side and your smiling side the best."

> # Who decides whether you live as a playful and powerful Warrior? You do.
>
> ■ ■ ■

This hit me like a ton of bricks. I finally realized I definitely had to lighten up and remove all of the burdens I was carrying. I had to lighten my load. I had to get back to honoring who I was.

This revelation caused me to realize my playfulness was my power. When I was playful, it moved both myself and other people into positive action. How playful are you being?

When you think of the word *powerful*, what images come to mind? Having great power or strength. Having a strong effect on people's feelings or thoughts. Having a strong purpose and living openly with understanding and vulnerability.

Personal power is the efficiency and ease with which you influence and control yourself. Your personal power produces the results you choose to have. The power of a single thought or action is able to change the course of your life. That is a lot of power and is a powerful way to live. It is all there inside of you and always has been. It is the power to have and achieve anything you desire. It is how you are. Powerful.

When you realize that you are able to manifest your desires quickly and definitively and you go after them directly, it is a powerful experience. It may be a while before you get used to the reality in which your desires manifest quickly and strongly. Consequently, it is tempting to redirect your power into creating false delays and phony obstacles so you are able to satisfy yourself with the illusion of progress. It requires practice to keep redirecting your personal power toward your desires.

Sometimes you may fear the consequences of your own personal power. What this means is that your own fear may prevent you from embracing your personal power for positive gain. You may also fear the responsibility that comes with your personal power. Understanding how powerful you are and using your power for creating positive gain requires responsibility, and sometimes this may seem scary. Warriors understand their personal power and use it responsibly. Turn your fear of personal power into positive purpose for you and for others. Embrace it, honor it, and live it.

In the past, I had the perception that if I showed my feelings, emotions, or vulnerabilities, I was simply being weak. Over the years, I buried my feelings and emotions deep down inside of me.

After going to a "Warrior" empowerment weekend, the light came on for me. I realized I was always vulnerable, regardless of whether I shared my feelings, emotions, or weaknesses. What I also discovered was that by burying my feelings, I was actually being weak. Although I was perceived as being tough or strong externally, internally I was weak.

Being vulnerable and being open is being powerful. I had it totally reversed. A Warrior's powerful self is derived from being open, authentic, and vulnerable. Warriors are open to their own vulnerabilities and feelings, whether it is emotional, physical, or spiritual. They see and embrace their vulnerabilities and openness as strengths instead of weaknesses.

Since that time, I have become more open and in touch with my innermost feelings and vulnerabilities. I have also been open to sharing them. This has caused my true power to shine. I now choose to see my vulnerabilities and openness as strengths.

Being playful *is* being powerful.

■ ■ ■

Throughout history, "warriors" have been defined as fierce soldiers and aggressive slayers and conquerors. They have been described as overbearing and dominating, overly rational, and overly sensitive as well as being cold, calculating thinkers who used their emotions to manipulate those around them—morally bankrupt soldiers of fortune who fought indiscriminately for trophies, glory, or money. Today, these old ways are counterproductive to living a vibrant and authentic Warrior life.

Today's Warriors possess the same great vigor and courage that define soldiers on the battlefield. They apply it in business, athletics, or everyday life. They engage energetically in an activity, cause, or conflict—and they do so *in a peaceful manner.*

One of the earliest definitions of "warrior" comes from the Chinese characters known as Kanji, which are used in the modern Japanese writing system. The first character of the Kanji word for warrior (か) means "conflict." The second Kanji character (の) means "stop." When these two characters are brought together, the actual meaning is clear: "stop conflict and create peace." Hence, a Warrior restores the concepts of harmony, unity, and peace—the complete opposite of *conflict.*

Noble is the Warrior who professes peace. God tells us in Matthew 5:9, "Blessed are the peacemakers: for they shall be called the sons of God." And in Proverbs 15:18, He reminds us, "A hot-tempered man stirs up strife; the slow to anger calms a dispute."

Warriors are simply keepers of peace. Are you living and keeping the peace within you and for you? There is a profound difference with today's Warriors. Today's Warriors are individuals who strive for self-awareness and peace. They seek to come out of their own shadows or darkness and into their light. They honor themselves and the world around them.

Warriors tell the truth about who they are and live within their own inner truth. They strive to be their best selves and to live with integrity. They choose to find and live in their light.

Are you living in your light and honoring yourself? Are you living in the light without a mask and within your true, authentic self? Warriors provide support for each other and provide encouragement to help each other succeed. Warriors choose to walk the walk and, more importantly, live the walk and love the walk. Playful and powerful Warriors commit to integrating into their everyday authentic lives the steps, principles, values, choices, and actions that honor them.

> **Warriors are simply
> keepers of peace.**
>
> ■ ■ ■

Today's Warriors understand and are willing to share the deepest parts of themselves. It means they have trust. Warriors are willing to allow others beyond their outer layers and to respond with compassion and caring when they communicate their inner feelings.

Intimacy flourishes when you share the deepest parts of your feelings and vulnerabilities. Such profound sharing occurs when a foundation of trust is in place. A level of trust provides both the safety to peel back the layers and to choose the risk of becoming vulnerable with yourself and others.

> **Being vulnerable and being
> open *is* being powerful.**
>
> ■ ■ ■

When you are most vulnerable, your sensitivity threshold is amplified. When your deepest core is exposed, you are likely to be much more sensitive. Warriors learn to accept, embrace and honor their sensitivities, core needs, and vulnerabilities. Start by asking yourself these questions: Are you open and being vulnerable? Do you ever share your deepest layers? When you are ready and when you feel emotionally safe, bring these questions into a dialog with yourself.

The power to see, hear, and feel life is at your fingertips and in everything you do. Live a life from your playful and powerful self. You have the opportunity to look with complete honesty at the life you have created. You are able to have profound choices for yourself and about what you choose to keep, what you choose to accept, what you choose to expand, what you choose to embrace within, what you choose to let go of, and what you choose to honor for yourself.

Your journey is a lifelong process. Embrace it and enjoy your great Warrior adventure.

**Are you ready to be the playful
and powerful Warrior you are?**

■ ■ ■

WARRIOR ACTION STEPS

■ ■ ■

THE PLAYFUL AND POWERFUL WARRIOR

You Are A Powerful Warrior; Live Playfully.

1. Reflect upon how your family, friends, coworkers, and associates respond to your playfulness. Choose to incorporate playfulness into your daily life. List three areas you are able to do so.

2. Are you living playfully and having fun? List three things you are able to do to embrace your fun and playful self.

3. Are you living within your personal power? List three things you are able to do to increase your own personal power.

4. Are you able to be vulnerable with others, sharing your deepest desires and fears? List what are you able to do to be more vulnerable with yourself.

5. Warriors are keepers of peace. Are you keeping the peace within you? List three things you are able to do to keep the peace within you.

■ ■ ■

Be Bold, Be Playful, Be Powerful, and Enjoy Your Great Warrior Adventure!

CHAPTER FOUR

■ ■ ■

Find and Live Your Purpose

A Warrior's purpose in life is a life of purpose.

■ ■ ■

When I was at the point of depression and suicide, I had stopped pursuing my purpose. I had simply lost sight of it. By the grace of God, I was able to once again see my true, authentic self. I was able to see, find, and start living my purpose. Through all of my struggles, I was able to find it, see it, and start living it.

Previously, I shared how my dream and vision came to light for me. Even though a great deal of my purpose in life was revealed, at that time I chose to ignore some of it and was unclear about how it would come together for me. It was at that time that I began to look deeper into what my purpose was. Since that time, my purpose has become much clearer, and I have chosen to accept it, honor it, and live it. Even when I began the new path of pursuing my purpose, I experienced many encounters that created some perceived roadblocks and exits. Through it all, I remained focused on my purpose once I became clear with it. I ask you to look deeper within yourself to find your clarity of purpose.

Those who seek will find. Whatever you look for, you will find. Choose time to think, to reflect, to connect with yourself, and to find your purpose. You have the ability to find and live your purpose.

Warriors know their purpose. Warriors live intentionally and with purpose, on purpose and for purpose. Living with purpose and with intention is one of the most powerful ways to live and love life.

A strong purpose with focused intention creates a powerful energy force. This power allows the Warrior to surmount many challenges and difficulties. Purpose creates a resistance to temptation and distractions, and creates a focus for staying the course.

When you are inspired by a great purpose, your thoughts, words, and actions create positive movement and synergy. Your mind transcends, and your consciousness expands in every direction. You find yourself in a new, exciting, and wonderful world. Dormant abilities, gifts, and talents will start to come alive, and you will discover yourself to be the great Warrior you are.

Are you living with and for your purpose? What is your purpose? Someone once said there are two great days in life: the day you are born and the day you discover your why. Warriors have discovered their why and know why they are here on earth. Knowing their purpose in life provides them stability. When others around them start abandoning their causes and giving up when life gets tough, Warriors use this assurance to steady themselves and ride out the storm. Warriors use their purpose as anchors in their lives, creating a confidence within themselves and for others around them.

God has given each of us a purpose for living life. Have you discovered your purpose? Have you identified what you are made of and what you are made for?

Be willing to stop going, doing, and chasing; start spending more time being and accepting who you are. Consciously connect with the original magnificence and essence of who you are.

> ## Warriors live intentionally with purpose, on purpose, and for purpose.
>
> ■ ■ ■

Warriors live a life with intent. To find your purpose is to find what you love to do the most. It is living with passion and searching for what gives your life meaning. It is all about being in tune with who you truly are and living a life of purpose. Expanding your awareness of who you are helps you to evolve.

Many people are on quests for acquiring tangible items and riches. They may appear to be living with purpose and may actually be doing so. They may also view this as their purpose. Their purpose is much greater than this. Tangible items and riches are simply tools used by Warriors to assist in fulfilling their purpose.

In the past, I got caught up in thinking my purpose was to simply acquire as much as possible. I became very good at it and enjoyed the associated challenges. Through this mindset, I simply lost my way. Over time I became dissatisfied with life and then myself. I realized it was okay to have nice things and to have great life experiences. What I found to be most important was having and living a godly life with purpose.

Many others live their lives by accident. They simply stumble into relationships, wander into careers, search for meaning, hope, and pray they will get lucky in love and find their fortune. They simply meander down their paths of life without purpose.

You are meant to live your life with purpose. I had to learn the hard way that my purpose was much bigger than me. Once I recognized this, I was able to design a life built to empower many more people than just me.

A friend and business partner, Nick Sarnicola, recently shared with me a story about a discussion he had with his fiancé, Ashley.

When the discussion was complete, he asked her one question: "What are we playing for?" What he was asking was this: "What is our end game? What is our overall mission and purpose, and what are we focusing on?" He knew that by being clear on their purpose, the little things and potential distractions along the way would simply fall into place. What are you playing for?

Imagine your life as ideal in every sense and in every area. I invite you to live your life with purpose. Be clear on what you are playing for starting right now.

How do you discover your purpose in life? Consider this story: One day, a master martial artist asked the famous actor and martial arts instructor Bruce Lee to teach him everything he knew about the art of warfare. Bruce held up two cups, both filled with liquid, and said, "The first cup represents all of your knowledge about martial arts. The second cup represents all of my knowledge about martial arts. If you choose to fill your cup with my knowledge, you must first empty your cup, of your knowledge."

To discover your true purpose in life, you must first be willing to empty your mind of all the false purposes you have collected or have been taught. To discover the purpose of your life, you have to allow yourself to be drawn to what you really love. Simply put, you have to *know* yourself and what you are passionate about.

Herein lies the beauty and simplicity of the entire process. Open yourself up to embracing what you love to do and are passionate about. Then it just happens. When it does happen, powerful, beautiful, and magnificent things come flowing forth for you. While it does require some patience and discipline to discover your purpose, the process of connecting the dots is easy. Your brain simply combines all of the input amassed over your lifetime, free from other interruptions, and computes the variables and outputs of all of your answers.

> **Knowing your life's purpose and fully living it creates great meaning and fulfillment.**
>
> ■ ■ ■

For most people, their everyday experiences and conventional reality monopolize their attention; people are distracted by everyday life and the challenges and distractions of education, earning a living, relationships, family, and health.

Are you wandering through life with little direction and plenty of daily distractions, hoping you will find a much happier life? There are far too many distractions to connect with yourself unless you change and focus on your environment. People are creatures of habit. Move away from what you are used to, and your mind will start thinking outside of your usual box.

One of the biggest obstacles to discovering your purpose is chronic busyness. Be clear and focused with your purpose. When you are permanently going, going, going, doing, doing, doing, it is a sure sign your busyness conceals a lack of clarity. It creates a fear of inadequacy, a feeling of unworthiness, and a lack of faith in your soul's ability to help you live your purpose. Be sure the way you are living lines up with your core values and priorities.

There are many things you are able to do today that will bring you more clarity on your life's purpose. How do you know what to focus on? The more open you are to this process, the faster it will work for you. Be clear. Identify your motivation, values, qualities, passions, gifts, and talents. Honor yourself by listening to what creates your feelings and desires to move purposefully through life.

Knowing your life purpose and fully living it creates great meaning and fulfillment. When you consciously align with your deepest reasons for being, you tap into rich reserves of energy, personal power, and passion. Your life begins to flow in new and delightful ways.

Visualize your life as you are living your passion right now. Your vision, when big enough, will excite you enough to choose to do something about it.

When you have imagined all of the paths available to you, ask yourself which one makes you feel the best. That path, which is truly yours to follow, will allow you to feel inspired, energetic, peaceful, and exactly who YOU are.

There are two primary paths you are able to choose in discovering your purpose. The first is passion. Passion is a great energizer. Warriors have a lot of positive energy. Warriors do what they love and love what they are doing. They always have plenty of energy, and they are excited to get on their way with their purpose. When you find your passion, you will find yourself with positive energy.

Steve Jobs, founder and CEO of Apple Computer, once said the following at a commencement address: "You've got to find what you love. And that is as true for your work as it is for your lovers. Your work is going to fill a large part of your life, and the only way to be truly satisfied is to do what you believe is great work. And the only way to do great work is to love what you do. If you haven't found it yet, keep looking. As with all matters of the heart, you'll know when you find it. And, like any great relationship, it just gets better and better as the years roll on."

What you love to do will give meaning and purpose for your life. What do you have the most fun doing? Warriors love the passionate journey as much as the destination. They have fuel in their tank because they have an incredible amount of passion.

Those who look within find what they are truly looking for. To find your purpose, look within. This is the point at which you determine and begin to live your purpose. It is choosing and honoring your actions. Listen to your gut feeling, inner voice, or intuition, and give yourself permission to go for it.

The second path is using your God-given talents, gifts, and strengths. What we often get the most joy out of is also what we are naturally good at. A major key to your happiness is to discover what you love to do and devote all of your energy to it.

> **Identify your life's purpose, and you'll have your own unique compass that will lead you to your true north every time.**
>
> ■ ■ ■

Find the path that enables you to answer the following questions: What do I do well? What are my strengths? What are my gifts and talents? What am I passionate about? What do I really care about? What am I compassionate about? What am I able to do right now to start using my passions, gifts, and talents? Warriors use their internal strengths to accomplish and to pursue their purpose.

When you have identified your direction, choose one baby step at a time. Stay true to your purpose, and honor yourself. Have faith in yourself. Choose to live a fulfilling life on *your* terms, with *your* values, and at *your* pace. Run *your* own race with *your* purpose. Live a life intentionally with purpose, on purpose, and for purpose.

What is your purpose, and is it bigger than you?

■ ■ ■

WARRIOR ACTION STEPS

■ ■ ■

FIND AND LIVE YOUR PURPOSE

You must be the change you wish to see in the world. —MOHANDAS GANDHI

1. What are your positive traits? What special talents do you have? List three of your talents. Ask those closest to you to help identify them. Are you imaginative, witty, or good with your hands? Find ways to express your authentic self through your talents and strengths.

2. What are your interests and what are you naturally curious about? What kind of learning do you enjoy? List three things you are interested in and enjoy doing.

3. What do you desire to change for the better in the world? List three things you would like to change in the world.

4. What are the things you currently enjoy doing, find most empowering, and are passionate for? What are the activities you feel most excited about? List all of the activities you choose to enjoy and are most passionate about.

5. What would you do if you had all the money you will ever require? What would you dedicate yourself to? Create a purpose statement around what you would do.

■ ■ ■

Be Bold, Be Playful, Be Powerful, and Enjoy Your Great Warrior Adventure!

CHAPTER FIVE

■　■　■

Place God First

To know God is to know thyself.

■　■　■

I had to reach the depths of despair and contemplate suicide before I was able to understand the true power of God. Because of the grace of God, I am able to share with you what I have learned. God grabbed hold of me and refocused me in finding and living my life's purpose. Had I originally put God first, the roadblocks and exit ramps I encountered would have been different. I have learned that by placing God first in my life, I am able to accept my magnificence and live a more fulfilling and purposeful life.

It is in God that the Warrior is able to discover his or her magnificent playfulness, power, and purpose. Warriors follow a higher calling—a spiritual calling—from God. They have faith and demonstrate it by the way they live their purpose for God. Warriors understand that they are called for something much greater than themselves.

God is calling you to be a part of something bigger than yourself. Do you sense there is something bigger out in the world for you to accomplish? God is calling you to trust Him and choose big steps of faith to create a significant difference in the world. The only way to find the ultimate purpose of your life is by responding to God's call to enter into a personal relationship with Him.

You are called to a personal relationship with God who created you. It is in God that you are able to discover your origin, your identity, your meaning, your purpose, your significance, and your destiny. Every other path leads to a dead end. God created you and accepts you no matter what you have ever done or failed to do.

We were designed to put God and His purposes first because God created all of us to have a relationship with Him. Genesis 1:27 tells us that "God created man in His own image, in the image of God He created him; male and female He created them." God loves you with an everlasting love and has a wonderful purpose for your life right now and for all of eternity. In John 10:10, Jesus said, "I came that they may have life, and have it abundantly."

The purpose of your life is far greater than your own personal fulfillment, your peace of mind, or even your happiness. It is far greater than your family, your career, or even your wildest dreams and ambitions. When you choose to know why you were placed on this planet, you must begin with God. You were born *by* His purpose and *for* His purpose.

Now think about this for a moment. God created you in His own image. God bestowed upon you unique qualities for you to use in your life and to assist others. Because you are in God's image and likeness, you have magnificence within you. Are you using your own magnificence and allowing it to shine? What is holding you back from letting your own magnificence shine through?

As I shared earlier, Coach Dale Brown always encouraged me to "Let God take care of the rest." When I started to tell my friends and associates that I was going to write a book, several people shared with me the following: "When you place God first, everything else falls into place."

After hearing this from several people, I started to think further about this. Then one day my assistant, friend, and future wife, Alita, said, "When you place God first, everything *does* take care of itself." It clearly made sense. This was the impetus for this chapter. When we place God first, everything else falls in place for us.

I grew up going to church and hearing how I should place God first. However, I had such a strong will and confidence, I would always place what I wanted first over whatever I thought God may have wanted. I always thought I knew what was best for me and I that could do what I wanted for me. I acted as my very own God. God honored that. He honored me and allowed me to use my own free will how I saw fit.

Looking back, I realize that I made some poor choices and decisions, decisions I would choose differently now that I allow God to guide my life. I have had many life challenges and struggles. Through it all, God has continued to accept me and love me regardless of the decisions I have made in my life. I learned that my plans will always be superseded by His plans.

I share this because if I had placed God first, I would have made decisions that would have honored both God and myself. I would have created better circumstances for myself. I was living a life of "Let's make a deal, theology." I would periodically make deals with God. All I was doing was actually manipulating what I wanted and what I wanted from God.

God knows what is best for me and what lies ahead for me. He even told me this in Jeremiah 29:11: "For I know the plans I have for you, says the Lord, to give you a hope and a future." Once I started to embrace this, I learned to be happy and have acceptance of the magnificent human being I am. I also began to see how God taught me what *worked for me*. He opened my eyes to seeing things differently, which gave me the ability to choose differently with His love. He has done the same for you.

> **When we place God first, all other things fall into their proper place.**
>
> ■ ■ ■

Begin with yourself. Realize you are a powerful, spiritual, and magnificent being, created in God's image. You are able to choose and create with love. Choose your thoughts and feelings, and have them reflect the positive and magnificent you. Choose all your actions with love.

Warriors understand that they are spiritual beings. When you begin to believe your true identity is a spiritual being and you are so much more than a body, your entire life begins to change. Seeing the essence of spirit and light in another person allows you to let go of your own bodily focus. You are able to recognize the same essence in yourself. This profound transformation unites you in oneness with God, who created you.

God built value into you when He created you. You are His ultimate creation. This is so powerful. Read this to yourself a few times: "I am God's ultimate creation." Wow! How does that resonate within you?

We are all God's creations. He has our best interest and chooses to have us truly shine and live with our true magnificence. All you have to do is put God first. Embrace Him, allow Him into your life, and everything else *will* fall into place.

Matthew 6:33 reads:

> Seek first His kingdom and His righteousness, and all these things will be added to you.

Let us all do as the above scripture says. Trust God and have God show and lead the way. Listen for God's voice in everything you do and everywhere you go. He will keep you on track when you allow Him to.

I invite you to always ask God to help you when making decisions. God chooses you to be blessed and have abundance. Since you are God's ultimate creation, give Him the trust and faith for your life. God has placed magnificent value inside of you. God created you and He also made you a powerful creator. He made you to be a Warrior for Him.

Genesis 1:26-28 reads:

> Then God said, "Let Us make man in Our image, according to Our likeness; and let them rule over the fish of the sea and over the birds of the sky and over the cattle and over all the earth, and over every creeping thing that creeps on the earth."

> God created man in His own image, in the image of God He created him; male and female He created them.

> God blessed them; and God said to them, "Be fruitful and multiply, and fill the earth, and subdue it; and rule over the fish of the sea and over the birds of the sky and over every living thing that moves on the earth."

Made in God's image, we are both valuable and valued beings—intelligent, aware of our surroundings, and capable of changing them. We are also morally aware and able to control our thoughts, words, and actions for higher purposes. God has given humans free will, which likewise reflects God's image. All men and women have the ability to choose for themselves their thoughts, words, and actions.

I am God's ultimate creation.

■ ■ ■

Say this to yourself and embrace it: "With the assistance of God, I am and have value. Great value! Magnificent value!" Say this to yourself again. Do you see the intrinsic value God has placed in you and upon your life?

> "The path of the righteous is like the light of dawn
> that shines brighter and brighter until the full day."
> —Proverbs 4:18

You are able to receive God's blessings. By having faith in God and acting boldly, unseen forces will come to your aid. Every act of faith and bravery increases your courage and capacity. His desire is for you to have faith and to be a willing and humbling servant.

Place God's will first, and be prepared for the amazing to occur for you. Simply have faith in Him. Always remember Hebrews 11:6, which says, "And without faith it is impossible to please Him, for he who comes to God must believe that He is a giver of those who seek Him."

God's magnificence is limited by the limits you set. He has all of the resources, power and willingness to give. Matthew 7:7 reads: "Ask, and it will be given to you; seek, and you will find; knock, and it will be opened to you."

God desires to have you be blessed. To bless in the biblical sense means to ask for or to impart supernatural favor. We are asking for the magnificent goodness that God has the power to know about you. When you seek God's blessing as the ultimate value in life, you are accepting His will, power, and purposes for you. All other needs become secondary to what you really desire.

God is choosing to work in us, through us, and around us, for His glory. Be open to His blessings, and your life will become marked by miracles.

Warriors have faith. Faith is a state of mind. Have faith in God. Have faith in yourself and faith in the infinite. Faith is the "eternal elixir" that gives life, power, and action to the impulse of thought.

Faith is the basis of all miracles and all mysteries. Faith is the element that transforms the ordinary vibration of thought, created by the finite mind of man, into the spiritual equivalent. Faith is the only element through which the spiritual force of infinite intelligence is able to be harnessed and used by man. Having faith creates many positive thoughts that will immediately come to your attention. Faith, obedience, and listening to the voice of God within you will allow you to experience many powerful and amazing results.

How does a Warrior of faith begin his prayers? The Prayer of Jabez is a good example.

> Oh, that You would bless me indeed,
> And enlarge my territory,
> That Your hand would be with me,
> And that You would keep me from evil.
> —1 Chronicles 4:9–10

Everything required to please God is found in His word. Are you willing to choose a stand under the authority of God? Are you willing to place your faith in God and learn what He would have you do with your purpose? Start living a purposeful life by placing God first. God is a patient God. He asks you to do the same and have faith in Him. Be patient, be faithful, and great things will happen for you.

Are you placing God first in your life?

■ ■ ■

WARRIOR ACTION STEPS

■ ■ ■

PLACE GOD FIRST

If they obey and serve Him, they will spend the rest of their days in prosperity and their years in contentment. —Job 36:11

1. Accept that you are God's ultimate creation. Say to yourself, "I am God's ultimate creation!"

2. Because you are in God's image and likeness, you have magnificence within you. Are you using your own magnificence and allowing it to shine? Is there anything holding you back from letting your own magnificence shine through? If so, list what it is.

3. Ask God to show you how you are able to use your magnificent God-given talents. List three of the most powerful talents you have.

4. Pray for God to come into your life, and pray that you will always keep God first. Routinely pray "The Prayer of Jabez" found in 1 Chronicles 4:9–10.

5. Everything required to please God is found in His word. Are you willing to choose a stand under the authority of God? Are you willing to place your faith in God and learn what He would have you do with your purpose?

■ ■ ■

Be Bold, Be Playful, Be Powerful, and Enjoy Your Great Warrior Adventure!

CHAPTER SIX

■ ■ ■

Forgive Your Internal Warrior Self

Forgiveness is a reversal of judgment.

■ ■ ■

Upon living with the experience I had with depression and contemplating suicide, I was faced with my own hurt and shame. I realized I created all of it for myself. I was at a point in my life where to move forward, I had to begin the process of forgiveness to heal and to fully love again. I knew that to regain my true, authentic Warrior self, I had to forgive myself.

Forgiveness provides the freedom to create a new future beginning right now. Warriors understand the power of forgiveness and love. Both are imperative for living as a playful and powerful Warriors. Forgiving completely, a Warrior is able to have inner peace and to love fully. Warriors understand that to experience complete peace of mind, forgiveness must be one of their primary functions.

The word "forgiveness" is built on the root word "give." To forgive means to "give up" and to let go. Forgiveness means choosing to let go, move on, and create positive healing in your life. When you forgive, you are willing to let go of resentment, revenge, and obsession. Forgiveness helps you move forward in life and is the key to your own happiness.

I had an experience with several people who had done some very unscrupulous actions within our business and toward me. My first reaction was to go after them. I had many thoughts of what I wanted to do. I simply wanted to retaliate. I had "eye-for-an-eye" thoughts, and I wanted to lash out and make a wrong a right. I wanted to get back at, get even, and get ahead. I wanted revenge.

I had vivid dreams and visions of what I wanted to do to get back at these people. Then I realized that if their poor behavior was the primary determining factor for my healing, then they would retain power over me indefinitely. I learned that a vindictive mindset creates bitterness and allows the betrayer to claim one more victim—and that victim was going to be me.

I realized I was upset with them, and I was upset with myself for allowing myself to be in that particular situation. I was also upset for continuing the relationships when I knew they were unhealthy for me. I learned that as long as I held on to this, I was in bondage to the past. It was keeping me from moving forward and living in the present.

At the time, I was going to my coach and anger management specialist, Jerry Medol. He showed me how to channel my hurts, anger, and negative feelings into positive releases. He showed me how any feeling, good or bad, positive or negative, was all right to experience. He said, "Embrace, accept, and release it." He also shared with me how the mind is unable to know the difference between something that has actually happened or is only a thought within the mind.

Because I was struggling with intense feelings, emotions, and visions, Jerry counseled me on what I could implement as a way to accept and come to terms with all this. Jerry encouraged me to embrace and lean into the strong feelings, emotions, and visions, to honor them and look at where they were rooted within. Since Jerry also understood I had no intent in acting on any of my intense emotions, feelings, and visions, he asked me to embrace these feelings and visions and always let them go after the fact. He taught me to say, "This is what I could do; however, I choose to forgive," and to say a prayer for both myself and for the other party. "I forgive you, and, more importantly, I forgive myself." He also recommended I thank those who have crossed me for the lessons I learned.

I knew I had to forgive and honor those and love them for who they were. I realized they were acting out of their own modeled behaviors, frustrations, fear, and hurt. I also had to honor and love myself. Once I started this process, I became more empowered. I focused on the healing and the lessons I had learned.

From that point on, I became free of the bondage I had placed myself in. I began to rejoice, for I was now free. I created my own peace of mind, and I created forgiveness for myself. I began to smile and laugh. More importantly, I began to let go of the negative feelings, emotions, and visions. I also started to embrace my inner Warrior self to a much higher degree.

Forgiving someone else is to agree to accept the wrong he or she has committed against you and to move on with your life. It means cutting the other person some slack and just letting go of the occurrence. As Alexander Pope once said, "To err is human; to forgive, divine." You know you have forgiven yourself or others when there is positive passage through your mind.

"What?" you say. "Cut them some slack after what they did to me? Never." Let go and move on with your life. The other people will have to answer for their actions at some point. They are creating their own internal toxicity and bondage and have to deal with what they have created for themselves.

Continuing a relationship after you choose to forgive is always your choice. The choice to forgive is always yours. It would be great if each party would come together and ask for forgiveness.

Accept the fact some people will choose to never forgive or ask for forgiveness. This is their choice. They have to live with their choices. Honor the situation and see it for what it is.

Forgiving eliminates the struggle and brings a sense of peace and well-being. It lifts anxiety and delivers you from depression. It enhances your self-esteem and gives you hope. The easiest way to find your flow and to go with the current of your life is to forgive.

> **You know you have forgiven yourself or others when there is positive passage through your mind.**
>
> ■ ■ ■

Since that time, I have become more empowered as a Warrior. I understand what happened, how it happened, and what I learned from it. I thank those people for teaching me powerful lessons in life. Their actions actually allowed me to choose to set myself free and to release myself from my own bondage.

It was also an example of how my own vine required pruning. A vine sometimes requires pruning to grow. This situation allowed me to grow. At the time, I was unable to see the reality of the growth that was to occur for me.

Now I live a more peaceful, fulfilling, and abundant life. The best part of this past experience is that I am now able to share and assist others how to heal their own hurts.

Are you in a similar position of having feelings that require setting free? Anyone who acts intentionally to harm another is trapped in his or her very own painful prison, even without being aware of or recognizing it as such. When you understand this, you are able to feel compassion instead of hurt, anger, or resentment.

One of the most lasting pleasures you will experience is the feeling that comes over you when you genuinely forgive another person. This happens whether or not the person knows about it. Forgiveness creates the freedom to create a new future beginning now.

Forgiveness releases the toxicity from your body and washes the slate clean. It creates joy. It brings peace, and it sets all the highest values of love in motion. It releases others from your judgment and criticism. It also releases you from being imprisoned by your own negative judgments and criticisms.

Forgiveness is a creative act that changes you from a prisoner of the past to a liberated Warrior at peace with your memories. It involves accepting the promise *right now*. Your life is far more promising than dwelling on memories of past hurts. To live in the now, you must first let go of the past. Why carry the weight of the burden of being unforgiving on your back? Do you enjoy the added weight?

Forgiveness is an internal matter. It is the experience of finding peace within yourself. When you choose to forgive, you are forgiving yourself. It is something you do for yourself. The spiritual purpose of forgiveness is self-healing, and it is a gift to yourself. Forgiveness is healing for you. The healing is letting go of fear and negative, hurtful thoughts from the past. You have the ability to correct your misconceptions and to remove the inner obstacles of peace. This begins with a willingness to find another way of looking at yourself and the external world.

It is discovering the effects you create for yourself when you hold on to your hurt, anger, fear, personal grievances, blame, condemnation, and victim consciousness. Feeling out of balance with life, or feeling out of control, stuck, weak, stressed, or disempowered is a sign that you are in victim consciousness. You are empowered to remove these shackles and make the choice to set yourself free. Your hurts will only heal when you forgive. You are then able to fully love with forgiveness.

> ## A Warrior is a keeper of peace, and forgiveness creates peace.
>
> ■ ■ ■

There are several common forgiveness misconceptions:

1. Forgiveness has to be something you give to someone else.

2. Something must be deserved or earned, and sometimes must be withheld, from the one who has done something wrong to you.

3. Forgiveness depends on whether the person who did you wrong or treated you badly apologizes or changes his or her ways.

4. Forgiveness is difficult because it is a sacrifice, like giving in, giving up, or losing your rightness. It discounts the pain you feel.

5. Forgiveness is sometimes thought of as letting someone who hurt you off the hook and no longer holding them accountable for their actions.

6. Forgiving the "offense" means you condone it. In fact, you are only forgiving what you know to be wrong for you—having to reconcile with someone who did you wrong or treated you badly. Telling someone you forgive them is simply a bonus.

Forgiveness is a shifting of attention away from the hurtful act. It is a release of the hurtful act for you. Research has shown that people who are deeply and unjustly hurt by others are able to heal emotionally and, in some cases, physically, by forgiving their offender.

Refusing to forgive by holding on to your hurt, anger, resentment, and offenses against you may create your own life miseries. The person you have never forgiven continues to be the victor and have power over you. The act of refusing to forgive has been considered a contributing factor to stress, physical illness, excess weight, financial scarcity, failed relationships, and a host of other challenges. When you are at war with yourself or with others, peace will evade you.

As long as you are holding onto your hurt, anger, resentment, and grudges against yourself or another person, you are poisoning your body with toxicity. It lowers your immunity toward illness. It affects your everyday life. On many levels, it also generates negative thoughts, expectations, and attitudes. All these repel your highest magnificence. It keeps your peaceful inner light from shining through. Remember that a Warrior is a keeper of peace.

Forgiveness breaks the cycle of hatred, resentment, anger, and pain, and this effect is often passed on to those around you. Forgiveness helps you make peace with your past and enables love. Love is the true source of power. As you forgive, you embrace your powerful Warrior life force.

Forgiveness is actually a simple process. Your ego creates the illusion of appearing to be complicated to forgive. Your ego dares you to imagine a better life, one that is based on blessed possibilities. Forgiveness eliminates your destructive thoughts about the particular situation and allows you to believe in the possibility of a better life.

> **Where there is forgiveness, there is love. Love and forgiveness go hand in hand.** —LESTER EARL
>
> ■ ■ ■

You are able to survive the pain and grow from it. Forgiveness and love are stronger than anger and resentment. The act of forgiveness and recovery from an offense may require some time to heal. It may be momentary, or it may be days, weeks, months, or even years. Instead of mentally replaying your hurt and focusing on it, forgiveness helps you focus your energy on the healing process. Simply identify a situation to be forgiven, and ask yourself, "Am I willing to waste my energy any further on this matter?" If the answer is no, then that is it. Simply let it go and forgive yourself— and all is forgiven.

Forgiveness allows you to let go of the pain in your memory. When you let go of the pain, you are able to have only the memory. You control your memory. When memory controls you, you are a slave to the past.

It is okay to have the memory as long as you have let go of the pain of the memory. When you allow it, time and choice are able to dull the vividness of the memory of the hurt. In many cases, the memory will eventually fade.

Always remember that you are human. Sometimes people do and say hurtful things. Focus on what you control—your thoughts, your words, and your actions. It is important to focus on what you are able to learn from these types of experiences.

> ## Who has the power to forgive? You do.
> ■ ■ ■

Do you choose to have peace of mind? Forgive. The energy you use to hold onto being unforgiving is the same energy you use to create peace and harmony for yourself. Focus your energy to move forward with forgiveness. Forgiveness is the single most important process to bring peace to your soul and harmony to your life.

Healthy relationships are only possible with forgiveness. You will only have a loving and rewarding relationship with yourself and with others by choosing peace with past significant others, your parents, your children, your friends, your associates, or anyone who you think may have done you wrong. This will improve your ability to have a healthy relationship with yourself or anyone else. It is only possible to truly be present and available to a new relationship by healing your hurt of the past.

> ## Forgiveness is healing for you.
> ■ ■ ■

Practice constant acts of kindness and you bring kindness to the world. Forgiveness is the most powerful act of kindness you are able to choose for yourself. This activity promotes unity, harmony, peace, oneness, and love. Warriors know true forgiveness is a choice they make entirely for their own peace and personal well-being. Are you willing to focus on offering forgiveness to a person who has hurt or wronged you? It is your choice. You have the power to forgive. Reclaim your personal power and simply forgive.

In your heart and spirit, you are a beautiful person with magnificence. Is there anything so unforgivable that it should keep you connected to an emotional bondage with another person or condition?

After forgiveness, comes love. Forgiveness is anchored in unconditional love. Forgive any past hurts right now, and embrace your love and live your life to the fullest. Be the Warrior you are and forgive.

Whom or what do you need to forgive?
■ ■ ■

WARRIOR ACTION STEPS

■ ■ ■

FORGIVE YOUR INTERNAL WARRIOR SELF

Anything and everything is able to be forgiven. It is simply a matter of choice.

1. Pray for wisdom and forgiveness. Pray for help in releasing the hurts, anger, resentments, judgments, and expectations that you are experiencing in your life. List three things you can pray for releasing.

2. Practice self-forgiveness.

   a. Begin the forgiveness process by forgiving yourself. Create a list of all the things you hold against yourself.

   b. Write the following for each thing you desire to forgive about yourself: "I, [your name], forgive myself for _____." Then look at yourself in the mirror as you say these affirmations of forgiveness and self-love.

3. Let go of victim-conscious scenarios. Describe any and all situations you are still holding on to.

   a. Symbolically release what you just wrote: burn it, tear it up, bury it, or flush it. As you let it go, imagine that you are releasing the need to feel victimized and that you are now free of the pain.

   b. Describe the same scenario from the perspective that it was somehow a great lesson, gift, or turning point in your life that served you in some important way.

   c. Keep the second scenario of the lessons learned and read it every day for at least a week. Reflect upon this so that you end up finding, embracing, and accepting the lesson for you.

4. Forgive others. As long as you are blaming anyone else for anything, you are giving away your power and creating more negative effects in your life.

a. Pray to God for help in stepping out of the hurtful dance you have created with this other person or situation.

b. Release blame, shame, and any idea you have done something wrong, and simply look at this situation as a mirror giving you important information about your core beliefs.

c. Are you allowing the poor behavior of others to be a primary determinant for your healing? Are you allowing them to have and retain power over you indefinitely? If so, list three things you are able to change right now.

■ ■ ■

Be Bold, Be Playful, Be Powerful, and Enjoy Your Great Warrior Adventure!

CHAPTER SEVEN

■ ■ ■

Always Come
from Love

**Love is patient, love is kind. It
rejoices with truth. It always
protects, always trusts, always
hopes, and always perseveres.**

■ ■ ■

ove is the answer. This is one lesson to learn, accept, and
apply. The essence of being is love. Start by loving yourself
and others unconditionally.

As I previously shared, I was once at a point in life where I was
choosing to *not* love myself. I had set false expectations and
buried my feelings. My love was simply depleted. Because of
God's grace and unconditional love, I was able to return to a
place of love.

Had I been coming from a place of self-love, I would have avoided
much of the pain, fear, chaos, and shame I created for myself.
I have always known I was full of love and, on many occasions
in the past, I openly shared my love. However, because I was so
closed off at other times in the past, I chose to show or share my
love conditionally. I loved myself conditionally. I loved others

conditionally. I allowed my ego to show my love only when it was beneficial to me; when I felt I had other parts of my life in order, then I would share my love. It was all conditional love.

> # Teach only love, for this is what you are.
>
> ■ ■ ■

I was creating a separation from my authentic self. I was creating a hole in my wholeness. Once I realized this, I chose to make the necessary changes and have understanding. I found, as a Warrior, that it is okay to be vulnerable and love unconditionally. I found loving unconditionally to be one of the most powerful things I could do for myself.

Over the past several years, I have realized that by loving myself fully, completely, and unconditionally, I have chosen to openly share my love with myself and with others. Being vulnerable and choosing to come from love has been one of the most important decisions I have made for myself. I ask for you to openly choose love for yourself.

Love is truly the great emotion in life. The word *love* is used in numerous ways to capture the special connection that ties us all together as human beings. Warriors all have an innate desire to be loved and to be whole. Their lives are complete with love. Love is their essence, and being vulnerable opens them to love.

Each of us desires the experience of love. See how much the notion of love plays a part in our personal journey of life. We seek it in our families, relationships, careers, religions, hobbies, and even—at times—in nature itself. All the while, love is right within us, ready to be accepted and shared.

Unconditional love, or authentic love, is a dynamic and powerful energy that lifts you through the most difficult times. It is available at any moment. It requires practice and intent to allow this energy to fully permeate your daily experience. It begins with yourself. To know what true love is, you must first have self-love. In loving yourself, you allow the feeling to generate within you, and then you are able to share it with everyone and everything around you. That which you send out returns to you in greater measure or abundance.

> ## Are you living and coming from love in every moment of your life?
>
> ■ ■ ■

I invite you to look at how you feel toward yourself—physically, mentally, emotionally, and spiritually. Begin the journey of unconditional love starting right now. When you allow yourself to understand the impact your actions have on yourself and the external world, you realize the necessity of choosing a loving action. You have the power to correct conditions within as well as to affect the world in which you live.

There are so many ways to apply love in your everyday life. Start by first choosing to care for and love yourself. As an act of self-love, educate yourself and choose to care for your physical body. Keep your thoughts and feelings positive and loving. Nurturing yourself also teaches you how to nurture life around you.

Have you ever had a feeling of "being connected"? This feeling is also described as "being in your power," "being in your center," or "coming from a place of love." You are open, warm, and loving to others. You are also confident and centered in yourself. You have unconditional love and acceptance.

This powerful energy of unconditional love will fill you up, make you whole, and provide you with the happiness you choose to have. All Warriors choose to have unconditional love. Warriors intuitively realize unconditional love is what matters.

Unconditional love is many times so different from the kind of love you may have been taught or known all of your life. Your misconceptions of conditional love began in early childhood. You may have experienced it when you did all of the right things: when you were clean, quiet, obedient, and otherwise good, people showed love for you. They smiled at you and spoke in gentle tones. When you misbehaved, all those signs of love instantly vanished. In short, you were taught by consistent experience that love was and is conditional. You had to buy your love from the people around you with your words and behavior. This is conditional love and, in its purest form, it is an imitation or false illusion of love.

Most people spend an entire life attempting to fill up their emptiness with conditional love. All they achieve is an ever-deepening frustration, punctuated by brief moments of superficial satisfaction. Much of the unhappiness in your life is because of conditional love. You experience frustration as you desperately and hopelessly attempt to create happiness from a flawed foundation of conditional love.

Many times, conditional love results in an unbearable emptiness. This may compulsively lead to filling your emptiness with whatever feels good in the moment: money, anger, sex, alcohol, drugs, violence, power, and the conditional approval of others—all of which are addictions and a giving away of your true, authentic self.

Conditional love is the major cause of confusion, frustration, chaos, and anger. Anything you use as a substitute for unconditional love becomes a form of imitation love. Although imitation love feels good for a moment, it is temporary. Unconditional love has staying power.

Unconditional love, peace, and harmony are the mortal enemies of the ego. Peace comes from experiencing unity with yourself. Love and peace are so intertwined that they are always found together. You will have the experience of love encircling within when you have allowed peace within.

Choose to come into your love. Are you willing to love yourself? This is an *important step* for you. When you are all filled up with love, you are more resourceful, compassionate, and understanding of yourself. Both your mind and vision becomes clearer.

> # Am I coming from a place of love?
> ■ ■ ■

The following are two key elements for choosing to come into your love:

Awareness. Notice and be aware. Are you being aware? Are you coming from love? Are you open? Are you closed? Is the conversation in your head about connecting or separation? Is there compassion or judgment? Is there love or fear? What's going on?

Analysis. Analyze what created any separation or closing down. What's the real reason or root cause? Evaluate and analyze what you are able to do to come into your love.

What do you choose to have? Would you rather come from love or stay separate and disconnected? The desire to open yourself to love is a choice you have to make for yourself. Decide exactly what you choose to do or have. Once you know what you choose, visualize it as if it is in the here and now. It is your choice, and you have the power to choose.

What are you willing to do? The first key word here is *you*. It is what *you* choose to do for yourself to get *you* to love. It is your choice. The second key word is *willing*. "Willingness" holds a higher energy vibration, so even the willingness to come into love allows answers to arise. With intention, results will follow. Your truth moves positive energy and allows you to open up. Are you willing to speak your truth? Are you willing to trust and honor yourself?

Are you willing to love authentically? Within you is an unlimited supply of love, and you hold the key to its release. You control how much fear and doubt, anger and hate you allow in your life.

Who decides whether you come from love? You do.

■ ■ ■

Is it this simple? It truly is. *Love is a choice you are able to have every single moment.* All you have to do is choose so. Every time you are dealing with a challenge, situation, event, or person, ask yourself this question: "Am I coming from a place of love?" The key to asking this question is this: "Are you truly coming from love and your soul?" Where there is love, there is peace. When you come from love, you are choosing to honor your soul and spirit. When you are coming from your ego, you are avoiding your authentic self or coming from a place of love. Remember this: where there is ego, there is misery.

By coming from a place of love, every moment of every day is a new beginning. This is a powerful realization. The meaning held in this opens you to a new way of living and experiencing life. Each moment holds a new beginning of possibility and it allows your personal potential to shine through.

When you are clear and receptive to your own higher loving self, you are able to express love within yourself and to the world around you—and the world will reflect the power of love. Love is such a powerful force, especially when shared. As a Warrior, be the source of love, and always come from love.

Are you coming from a place of love?

■ ■ ■

WARRIOR ACTION STEPS

■ ■ ■

ALWAYS COME FROM LOVE

Forgiveness in your heart creates love.

1. Are you coming from love? Are you open? Are you closed? Is the conversation in your head about connecting or separation? Is there compassion or judgment? Is there love or fear? What's going on? List three things you are aware of from these questions.

2. Conditional love is the major cause of confusion, frustration, chaos, and anger. Anything you use as a substitute for unconditional love becomes a form of imitation love. List three areas where you are able to eliminate conditional love in your life. Analyze what has created any separation for you. What is the real reason or root cause? Evaluate what you are able to do to come into your love.

3. Start by loving yourself and others unconditionally. Look into a mirror and see yourself as if it is for the first time and say, "I love myself unconditionally." Say this again and again. Say it out loud.

4. Are you living and coming from love in every moment of your life? What are you able to do to come from a position of love? A great thing to do for yourself in any situation is to ask yourself, "Am I coming from a place of love?"

5. Love yourself and hug someone.

■ ■ ■

Be Bold, Be Playful, Be Powerful, and Enjoy Your Great Warrior Adventure!

CHAPTER EIGHT

■　■　■

The Ego

The ultimate aim of the ego
is to be something.

■　■　■

When I was at the very depths of life, I was living in fear and chaos, and I was full of pain and anger. All this was because I was living from my ego instead of coming from my spirit, my soul, my true, authentic Warrior self.

While I was going through anger management a few years ago, I realized that my ego was much larger than what I had thought. I realized how subtle it was in masking over my true, authentic self.

I was a former soldier in the U.S. Army, and I still acted as if I were in the military. I portrayed my strength externally. I thought my strength and power were things I had to display outwardly. All it was, though, was my ego. It was a false strength.

I realized I had two internal forces opposing each other. I simultaneously had love for people and life and was very critical and judgmental of myself and of others as well—all of which was my own self-projection.

When talking about others, I would first talk about my perceived negatives of them. I was focused on looking at their negatives versus looking at their strengths and magnificence. It was a constant yin and yang, back and forth, and I was oblivious to it.

When I realized what I was doing and how negative it was, I had to make some adjustments in my life to free myself from the shackles keeping me from having a completely free and fulfilling life every day. I chose to be more in touch with my true self and my spirit.

Have you ever felt there were two opposing forces inside of you, each pulling in opposite directions? One force simply loves life, people, and is always curious about exploring and experiencing the world. The other energy force is more protective, practical, cautious, and judgmental.

The first energy force is your *spirit*, or *soul*. This energy force is alive and free, creative, expressive, abundant, playful, powerful, and magnificent. This part of you guides you calmly and adeptly through new and challenging experiences. This is your true center, and it is always there for you to access. Spirit is your "life force energy" and is about experiencing, creating, expressing, and connecting to your true, authentic self.

The second energy force is *ego,* and it is always there for you to access as well. The ego is more like a bodyguard, a tour guide, and a protective covering or mask. This force desires to look good for others or, at the very least, to avoid looking bad. Ego likes to control, although it pretends otherwise.

The ego force views the world as a potentially harmful place and fears being hurt and exposed, remaining separate, and becoming isolated and closed off from others. It blames, criticizes, compares, and makes excuses. The ego also loves complex situations. *Should* is one of the ego's favorite words. This energy looks for answers from its mind and often confuses reality with fantasy. Living isolated within the confines of the body, it chooses to be cautious, safe, independent, complex, and *separate*.

The ego's job is to provide the appearance that the physical body is safe and that it is guiding your spirit through the journey of life. This is simply an illusion. Your experience of life and the world around you is based exclusively on what you sense and your interpretation of those inputs. Everything you see, everything you feel, and everything you know is based on your subjective interpretation of information fed to you by your senses. The ego masks your ability to find your true Warrior self. It also creates separateness from your true, authentic self.

Here is a story about how the ego operates. A small child was visiting his grandparents. When the grandfather was putting him to bed, the child suddenly started crying and said, "I want to go home. I am afraid of the dark." The grandfather said, "I know that at your home you sleep in the dark. I have never seen a light on. So why are you afraid here?" The boy replied, "Yes, that's right, Grandpa. That is *my* darkness. This darkness is completely unknown."

This is profound and real for many. You may feel secure within your darkness and insecure in an unknown darkness. Your darkness, your security, is false and is nothing more than an illusion. It is something to hold on to, and to cling to.

> **The ego masks your ability to find your true Warrior self.**
>
> ■ ■ ■

What is ego? Merriam-Webster defines "ego" as "the self especially contrasted with another self or the world." In psychoanalytic theory, it is one of the three divisions of the psyche (the id and superego being the other two) that serves as the organized conscious mediator between the person and reality—remembering, evaluating, planning, and responding to the physical and social world.

Sigmund Freud, who founded psychoanalysis, believed that the ego works independently of both the personality and the body. He theorized that it integrates these aspects of the person—as well as other aspects such as memory, imagination, and behavior—and mediates between the id and the superego by building up various defense mechanisms.

What is important to note is that the ego functions both in the "perception of" and the "adaptation to" reality. It is how you perceive yourself in relation to the world; in short, it is your self-esteem. Therefore, it is an accumulated phenomenon and by-product of living with others. It is a social need, a reflection of the external world.

How is the ego created and formed? A child is born. The child is you. You are born without any knowledge and any consciousness of your own self. When you are born, the first thing you become aware of is the existence of other people. Your five senses start kicking in. This is natural because your eyes open outwards, your hands touch others, your ears listen, your tongue tastes food, and your nose smells the external world. All these senses open outwards for you.

You become aware of your mother. Then, bit by bit, you become aware of your own body. You are hungry. You feel your body. This is how you, as a child, begin to grow. You mother smiles. She appreciates you. She says, "You are beautiful." She hugs and kisses you.

Through appreciation, love, and care, you feel you are good. You feel you are valuable. You feel you have significance. You feel good about yourself. A center is born. This center is a reflected center. It is an illusion of your real being. You become aware of what others think about you. Now an ego is born. Your ego.

In the beginning, your mother means the world to you. Then others will join your mother and the world goes on growing. The more the world grows, the more complex the ego becomes—because the opinions of others are now reflected onto you.

You then go to school and interact with others. The teacher will reflect onto you who you are. You interact with other children and they will reflect onto you who you are. You will have others reflect onto you. Bit by bit, everybody adds to your ego and everybody attempts to modify your ego in such a way so you can fit within the external world.

As a child, you are brought up to fit into the external world. Society creates an ego because the ego is able to be controlled and manipulated. You, the child, require a center; and you are completely unaware of your own center. Society gives you a center and you are, by and by, convinced that this is *your* center. It is your ego, given to you by the external world.

When you receive good grades, your parents are happy. They hug and kiss you and give you lots of attention. They say, "What a beautiful child. You are wonderful." They are establishing your ego, a subtle ego.

At some point, when you come home feeling dejected or unsuccessful, when you have failed to pass your exam, or after you spent the entire game on the bench, you start to feel rejected and unappreciated. You will work harder next time because your center feels shaken. Ego is frequently shaken and is always in search of food, of someone who will notice or appreciate it. That is why you continuously ask for attention. You get the idea of who you are from others. Others attempt to shape and mold your center. This center is false.

You actually have two centers. One center is God-given. This is the self, *your authentic self*. You are born with it, and it is *your* center. The other center, which is created by the external world, is the ego. It is a false thing, and it is an illusion.

Through the ego, you are allowing the external world to have influence over you. The external world acknowledges or appreciates you when you behave in a certain manner or code.

When the ego is unappreciated by the external world, your ego may waver. When the ego wavers, you may start to become unaware of where you are, who you are or what is going on with you. All of your boundaries may seem to disappear and you become confused and fearful.

Being afraid will cause you to fall back and to rely on your ego. When this happens, you will simply be confused and will continue to have challenges and chaos in your life. Because of these challenges and chaos, you may be afraid to lose the ego. You have to pass through the unknown or chaos before you are able to attain to your real center. This is where you will find true peace, *your true, authentic self.*

The ego is always looking to be fed.

■ ■ ■

When you are miserable, the ego feeds on your misery. Even being miserable provides you with a feeling of "I am secure." By moving away from it, fear comes over you, and you start to feel insecure or afraid of the unknown darkness and chaos. All because society has placed upon or managed to clear a small part of your being, your ego.

It is just like going into the woods to live. You make a little clearing, you clear a little ground, you put up a fence, you build a home, you grow a garden, and you are great. You have planned everything and everything is good. Beyond your fence is the woods: the wild and the unknown.

This is how it happens to your consciousness. The external world has made a little clearing in your consciousness and has cleaned just a small part, one completely fenced in. Everything seems to be good for you. The conditioning is just to clear a part so you feel at home.

In the small fenced-in area, you become insecure and afraid. Beyond the fence there appears to be more danger. However, you are the same as you are within the fence. Your conscious mind is just one part of your whole being, and the remaining parts are still waiting in the darkness. In the remaining parts are where your real center is hidden.

To get to your real center, you have to choose to move into the unknown with the fear of danger. This is where your real center is hidden. For a while, all boundaries may appear to be lost. For a while, you may feel disoriented, dizzy, confused, afraid, and insecure.

As a Warrior who is daring, courageous, and strong, you will go forward. This will prevent you from falling back to the ego. There is a hidden center within you that you have been carrying, and this is your soul, your true and authentic self. Once you come in contact with your soul, everything changes in a positive and bright way for you. This is done completely by you.

Now everything becomes a clearing *for you*. A new beginning, a world filled with security, peace, love, and your magnificence shines through. You arise into your true self—your authentic Warrior self.

Your true, authentic self or center is a flowering center within. It goes on flowering and living.

The ego is just like the difference between a real flower and a plastic or paper flower. The ego is a plastic flower. It just looks like a flower and may even feel like a flower. The real flower outside in the garden is eternal. A flower is something that blossoms. This plastic thing is lifeless. Are you satisfied with a plastic ego? An illusion? Your ego?

The ego has a certain quality. It is just like a plastic thing. It is very easy to receive it because others give it to you and you accept it. Ego is a social phenomenon, society's view of you. *It is an illusion of you.* It gives you a function and a hierarchy in society. When you remain satisfied with it, you will miss the whole opportunity of finding the self, your true, authentic self or center.

> ## Ego is a social phenomenon, and it is society's view of you.
>
> ■ ■ ■

Your ego creates chaos, misery, and fear. You may be unable to see all of the chaos, misery, and fear because of your own darkness. Your ego continuously comes in conflict with others because every ego lacks confidence about itself and requires feeding. It feeds on both positive and negative attention.

What is required to feed the ego is the attention of others. The ego is always looking for some trouble. The ego says this is good because at least the attention is being paid to me. Even having anger will be good for the ego because it will garner attention. The ego goes on finding causes to suffer.

In many ways, you attract the attention of others by the way you dress, look, act, or behave. When you understand what type of situation is there, you immediately change, just like a chameleon. You do this so people pay attention to you. It is an illusion, and it is your false self, your ego. This is a type of deep begging, and a real beggar is one who asks for and demands attention, which is what the ego does to be fed.

When others are paying attention to you and then they stop, you may become shaken. They had been paying attention to you—caring, loving, moving around you, and helping you feel that you were somebody. Your whole world may seem to be lost, and you are simply shaken. You were allowing them to give you the center. It was just the illusion of having your center; it was a false center.

This is how people become codependent on others, almost to the point of a deep slavery. Ego has to be a slave. It thrives and depends on others. The ego shows itself through various ways. Resistance, control, restriction, blaming, judgment, negativity, self-righteousness, the need for recognition, and fearfulness are all ways the ego disguises itself. The ego also expresses itself as being needy, which it is.

This is all a form of separating from your inner self and your magnificent power. It creates the illusion that *you* need something "over there" to complete you. In the movie *Jerry Maguire,* Tom Cruise's character says to his wife, "You complete me." This is clearly a false statement, because only you are able to complete you or make yourself 100 percent whole. The ego would like for you to believe something outside of yourself or "over there" is able to complete you. The ego has many faces, and they all focus on keeping you separate from your true, authentic self.

We are all able to so see the ego in others. Many times, however, it is difficult to see our own ego. That is when the challenge arises. The ego is often hiding in *your* darkness or shadow. This is unknown territory. Since the ego is oftentimes subtle and very sneaky in its expression, it is important to recognize its nature and realize how it may be revealing itself in your life.

Self-consciousness is a reflection of the ego.

■ ■ ■

Cast your ego aside. To understand the ego as deeply as possible, you must allow your ego to slip away. To attain your true, authentic self, your ego must be cast aside. Eliminating the ego eliminates the slavery you have allowed for yourself. Understand this and begin to change your life.

Start looking for your ego. Looking for ego in others is none of your business; it's theirs.

Whenever you experience chaos, misery, or fear, immediately close your eyes, like you did when you were a child, and find out where the feeling is coming from. You will always find it is the ego, or false center, that has clashed with something or someone else. When your ego is shaken and you are in misery, just look inward and find out why. You may have to look in the shadows or underneath several layers of thoughts, issues, and feelings deep inside you.

External perceptions of causes are simply a reflection of what is inside of you. The basic cause *is within you*. You are modeled and taught to always look externally. Have you ever asked these questions: What is making me miserable? What is the cause of my anger? What is the cause of my fear?

When you look outside yourself, you will miss it. Just close your eyes and look within. The source of all chaos, misery, fear, and anger is hidden in *you*. Just like a mask, your ego covers your true, authentic self. When you find the source, it will be easier for you to move beyond it. You are able to see that it is your own ego that gives you trouble. When you understand your ego, you are able to eliminate the source of misery.

When you attempt to drop your ego, you will attain to a certain subtle ego that says, "I have become humble." Being humble is an illusion, too. The ego is simply in hiding. Humility is a shadow of your real center. When the ego is gone, a humility comes to you. The ego is so subtle.

A truly humble man is neither humble nor egotistical. He is just simple. He is unaware that he is humble. He is just being.

When you are aware you are humble, the ego is still present. Look at all the humble people. There are millions who think they are very humble. They have the subtlest egos lurking in their own shadows.

Humility is a source of food for the ego. It says, "I am humble," and then it looks at you and waits for you to appreciate it. "You are really humble," it would like you to say. See the smile that comes to its face when you tell it so.

Ego is a hierarchy that says, "Nobody is like me; I am the most humble man." This is how the ego operates. Its ways are so subtle and cunning that you have to be very, very alert. Only then will you see it. Just see that all chaos, misery, and fear, *all comes through the ego.*

> **The ego creates separateness from your true, authentic self.**
>
> ■ ■ ■

Just watch. When you attempt to drop the ego, you become the ego. It always comes back. Whatever you do, just stand back out of the ego and look and watch. Whatever you do, understand that humility and simplicity will do nothing to help you. These are all subtle signs of the ego. One thing is possible, and that is to just watch and see. Simply watch. If you say it is the source of all misery and you say it or repeat it, it then is projected and reappears.

Just be. Whenever you are miserable, just close your eyes and see where this misery is coming from inside you. You will find it, and it is your own ego. When you understand the ego is the cause, one day you will suddenly see that it has disappeared. The very understanding that the ego causes all misery becomes the beginning of the dropping. Understanding and just being is the disappearance of the ego.

Here is a good illustration of how many of us imprison our-selves with our ego because of our own actions. In a *Charlie Brown* cartoon, Charlie is making a house out of children's blocks. He is sitting in the middle of the blocks, building the walls. Then a moment comes when he is enclosed—he has walled himself in. Then he cries, "Help, help. Let me out." He has done the whole thing by himself and to himself. Now he is enclosed and imprisoned.

This is a childish example; however, this is all that you have done to yourself. You have made a wall around yourself, and you are now crying, "Help, help. Let me out." You have cre-ated your own perceptions of reality of your misery. As human beings, our reality is our perception and our interpretation of what it is. Everything we experience is filtered through our five senses. It is our consciousness of reality that determines how we view and interpret the world and give it meaning.

The whole path towards your true, authentic self has to pass through this territory of the ego. The false has to be under-stood as false. The source of misery has to be understood as the source of misery, and then it simply drops. When you are tempted to say, "I have dropped the ego," simply laugh at the irony of the whole thing. The joke is you are the creator of all your chaos, misery, and fear, and you still have an ego.

By having an understanding of the ego and how it works in your life, you are able to make adjustments to minimizing it. Then, and only then, is the ego able to disappear.

> ## The ego is the source of all chaos, misery, and fear.
>
> ■ ■ ■

Do you see your own ego? Just watch it. The more you watch, the more capable you will become. Suddenly one day you will see that it has dropped. When it drops by itself, only then does it completely drop. There is no other way. It drops just like a dead leaf from a tree. Just a breeze, a situation, and the dead leaf simply drops to the ground. The tree is unaware the dead leaf has dropped. It makes no noise and it makes no claim. Nothing. The dead leaf simply drops and falls to the ground just like that.

When you are fully aware and understand that your ego is the cause of all your chaos, misery, and fear, one day you will see the leaf has dropped. It will settle onto the ground and die of its own accord. When you see that it has simply disappeared, then your real authentic center arises. Imagine Buddha sitting under his bodhi tree. If the whole world suddenly disappears, will it make any difference to Buddha? No, because he has attained to his true, authentic center. An authentic Warrior is one who lives in himself and has a center of his own. He only depends on looking within himself to be centered.

Your spirit shows up when you let your thinking mind go. Let go of all your illusion of control. The only things you are able to control are *your thoughts, words,* and *actions.* Know you are whole and complete just as you are. Allow your spirit to guide you. The more you embrace this, the more peace you will have. Continue to be and live within your true, authentic self, and let your spirit shine.

What is ego versus spirit? Ego and spirit are two powerful forces. Many people continue to struggle between these two energies. Sometimes it may feel like you have split personalities. The more you are in touch with your spirit, the more in touch you are with your true, authentic self. The more you align yourself with your spirit, the more your ego will hide.

Below are ways to differentiate between your ego and your spirit. These are characteristics of the ego and its counterpart, the spirit. Separation is the common theme to each word set below. The ego strives to keep you separate from your inner self, and your spirit strives to keep you whole.

Ego		Spirit
Separation	vs.	Connection
Control	vs.	Letting Go
Mind	vs.	Heart
Victim	vs.	Choosing Responsibility
Excuses	vs.	Results
Should	vs.	Inspiration
Resistance	vs.	Acceptance
Restriction	vs.	Freedom
Confusion	vs.	Clarity
Suppression	vs.	Self-Expression
Worry	vs.	Anticipation
Uninspired	vs.	Creativity
Stressed	vs.	Peaceful
Frustrated	vs.	Resourceful
Protection	vs.	Vulnerability
Fear	vs.	Love
Laziness	vs.	Nurturing
Doubt	vs.	Trust
Scarcity	vs.	Abundance
Closed	vs.	Open
Shame	vs.	Acceptance
Apprehension	vs.	Courageous
Struggle	vs.	Flow

Understanding is the disappearance of the ego.

■ ■ ■

When you rely on something outside of yourself to feel good, be secure, or be happy, you are on the emotional roller coaster of life. Have you ever noticed that as soon as you "surrender," your solutions start to appear for you?

When you become more conscious about the nature of these forces, you access this all-knowing, wise, and powerful force in your life more consistently. The result is a life with *more* peace, joy, love, abundance, creative flow, and wholeness.

**Do you see in your life how
your ego is revealing itself?**

■ ■ ■

WARRIOR ACTION STEPS

■ ■ ■

THE EGO

Warriors know each perceived challenge, mistake, or failure is a lesson for them. Warriors embrace the lesson learned.

1. Recognize that you have an ego. What are three things you immediately recognize about your ego?

2. The ego is always looking to be fed. List three areas where your ego is seeking to be fed. Why is it seeking to be fed?

3. Have you ever felt there were two opposing forces inside of you, each pulling in opposite directions? List three times this has happened, and identify how you are able to be in more alignment with your soul/spirit.

4. Whenever you experience chaos, misery, or fear, immediately close your eyes, like you did when you were a child, and find out where the feeling is coming from. You will always find it is the ego, or false center, that has clashed with something or someone else. What chaos, misery, or fear are you experiencing? Are you able to identify where it is coming from?

5. Be aware of your motivation. Look at your motivation behind your thoughts, words, and actions. Be aware when your sense of well-being becomes linked to another's behavior.

■ ■ ■

Be Bold, Be Playful, Be Powerful, and Enjoy Your Great Warrior Adventure!

CHAPTER NINE

■ ■ ■

The Illusion of Control

All you control are your thoughts, words, and actions.

■ ■ ■

B ecause of my control issues, I created my own stress, chaos, and pain. One of my good friends and business partners Ryan Blair, CEO of ViSalus Sciences, once commented, "You are either in control or out of control." I was so busy attempting to control various parts of my life, plans, events, situations, and people that I became out of control.

How many things in your life do you attempt to control? Schedules, time, relationships, children, money, business transactions, performance, people's opinions and beliefs about you, clutter, your emotions, other people's emotions, your thoughts, level of fulfillment, stress, outcomes, your health, your environment, your future, and so forth. Does it seem like a lot of control is happening in your life? Attempting to control something or someone creates a lot of chaos and stress.

So what exactly do we mean by control? By definition, *control* means "to exercise restraint or direction over." You have most likely witnessed instances in which people attempt to dominate or command others, whether it is at home or in the workplace. You have also probably seen instances when someone, or a group of people, has attempted to eradicate an idea or prevent the growth or spread of a movement.

Many believe control is a necessity. Do you? Attempting to control anything outside your thoughts, words, and actions is an illusion. All you are able to control is *your* thoughts, words, and actions.

Why do you attempt to control? Control is a derivative of your ego. There seems to be two primary driving forces. You believe that control will give you something positive: more peace, self-esteem, financial gain, fulfillment, or sense of security. You use control as a defensive method to protect yourself, to avoid pain or discomfort, or to avoid confronting a fear or facing the unknown.

How do you control? There are a variety of ways in which control has the appearance of actually being in control. Instead of facing the unknown in your life, do you notice that creating to-do lists, making plans in advance, and staying busy provides you with a sense of certainty and security?

Control shows up in relationships as nagging, whining, emotional upset, anger, sadness, frustration, threatening, influencing, manipulating, use of force, negotiating, and seeking commitment. There are also passive ways to control, such as ignoring, avoiding, and emotionally withdrawing, which are equally potent. Even body language or "the look" can be controlling. More subtly, you may embellish or minimize the facts or become a "people pleaser" in an attempt to manage the perception of others.

When you know what to expect, it seems you are better able to feel at peace inside, right? However, this is a false sense of security and peace. Fundamentally, seeking control is an illusion of having true inner peace.

When you seek something outside yourself, it suggests that something is missing from your life. When you avoid something, it suggests something can be taken away. Both of these states create a sense of anxiety. While you ultimately desire peace of mind, striving for control creates the perception of what you choose to have. It is just an illusion of what you want.

> ## The only things I actually control are my thoughts, words, and actions.
>
> ■ ■ ■

What is your reality of control? Your actions influence reality. How many times have you planned and repeatedly confirmed the details, and then something else happened instead? People have committed their word and then—at the last minute—chosen to follow through with a different commitment. You worked diligently on a project, only to scrap it entirely and begin again or move on to something else. You created your to-do list, then found yourself doing something completely different that same day. These are examples of things you perceived to be in control of. How often do people, children, or animals do exactly what you expect and desire?

Do you ever find yourself caught up in emotions at inopportune times? However one plans, life is always unfolding. What would happen if you let go of control or loosened the grips of what you attempt to control?

Why let go of control? This may seem to be a big, scary question for many. First of all, when you loosen the grips of control, you are still able to arrive at the same outcome. Perhaps it could be something even better for yourself. Living with your flow is a much easier process for you. Find your flow and go with the current of your life.

One reason to let go of control is that it often impedes the very results you are seeking. In the face of control, others may pull away, become defensive, or disappear completely. Your actions may negatively impact another's self-esteem. Attempting to control often costs time and energy and leads to non-essential mindless chatter. It also causes stress, anxiety, and frustration when things unfold other than according to your plan. When you believe you require something outside yourself or that something may be taken away from you, you are choosing to be enslaved and are preventing yourself from living life freely.

Exploring the dynamics of control and loosening its grips will allow you to experience more of what you desire, more effort-lessly. Are you experiencing a sense of well-being in every area of your life? Start analyzing and investigating areas of attempted control to see if and where it is happening. The ego is forceful when it comes to being in control. It plays a more dominant role in your life and it suppresses your true spirit.

As Ryan Blair once stated, "You are either in control or out of control." Warriors focus on being and controlling the only things they do control—*their thoughts*, *words*, and *actions*.

What are you attempting to control in your life?

■ ■ ■

WARRIOR ACTION STEPS

■ ■ ■

THE ILLUSION OF CONTROL

**The key to becoming free of the
ego mind, with all its consequences,
is to become deeply conscious of
this present moment—the now.**

1. Simply let go of everything you attempt to control outside your thoughts, words, and actions. List three things you are attempting to control.

2. Surrender the illusion of control in one or more areas of your life. List three things you are able to surrender.

3. Notice how much you are attempting to identify future events so that you will feel more at peace. List anything you are attempting to control in the future.

4. What price are you paying in the illusion of control?

   a. Create a list of what the opposite behavior and/or freedom would look like.

   b. Create a list of what issues your control is creating.

   c. Create a list of what you fear may be taken away.

   d. Create a list of what you fear you are incomplete without.

5. Focus on what you do control, your *thoughts, words,* and *actions.*

■ ■ ■

**Be Bold, Be Playful, Be Powerful, and
Enjoy Your Great Warrior Adventure!**

CHAPTER TEN

■   ■   ■

Conscious Language: Manifest Your TRUE Desires

Think, say, and do what you choose to have. Understanding your conscious language will provide you with a roadmap for achieving your desires.

■ ■ ■

The thoughts you have and the words you speak directly affect everything in your life. Success, health, prosperity, relationships, and career are affected both positively and negatively. How many times have you set goals, visualized your desired outcome, created and repeated positive affirmations, and received a different result or outcome? There are numerous potential causes for this. Did you know you may be speaking in a self-defeating manner that subtly undermines your success and, in turn, enhances your chances of failure in the future?

When I first started to understand the consequences of my thoughts, words, and language, I could see how I had created both positive and negative events for myself. My conscious language created my own world full of both positive and negative results.

Have you ever heard the statement, "Be careful what you ask for, you just might get it?" It's a statement I am sure many of us have heard and are able to relate to. Simply put: ask and it is given.

> "And all things you ask in prayer, believing, you will receive."
> —Matthew 21:22

There have been many books written on the subject of conscious language, the power of positive thinking, and the law of attraction. Conscious language is a main function of both the power of positive thinking and the law of attraction. The concept is that you must master your conscious language and you will master the law of attraction, which focuses on what you desire. It is understanding and focusing on how you use your thoughts and words and how you place them into action to attract what you desire.

If you are a person who believes in God and prays to God, it is extremely important that as you study conscious language, the power of positive thinking, and the law of attraction, you make sure you include your beliefs in the formula.

Further study on this subject will provide more depth and understanding than what I will cover in this book—and I highly recommend that you do research the topic. For now, understanding and applying the basics I cover will assist you in embracing your true Warrior self—and have a positive impact on your life.

Some may ask, "Where does God fit into the law of attraction?" What the appropriate question is, "Where does the law of attraction fit in with God"?

The answer is quite simple and profound. God has given us the law of attraction through his word. Many people believe the law of attraction is "New Age" or something new. This law has been around since the beginning of creation. As I began to understand that God is the supreme creator that abides by this same law, He has power over the law and lives in complete perfection of it . . . because it is a perfect law, designed perfectly to support us in our experience of learning through our life here on earth.

God created the universe, and the universe works by laws. The law of attraction, or what is also called the law of creation, is in operation in every sphere of the universe.

God created us out of an immense joy in the act of creation and gave us "free will" to then, with joy, watch us create for ourselves the lives we have chosen, both consciously and unconsciously. Along this journey, He has given us teachers and angels to help and protect us. God created the law of attraction.

What this means is that when you have a desire (a thought), the energy is sent out into the universe, and your consciousness makes this work. The energy is God, and God is our collective consciousness. God, our creator, loves us in such a way as to give us unlimited abundance and to feel immense joy at our receiving these gifts and of our giving abundantly to each other. It is through immense faith and belief, fueled with the power of our minds and emotions, that the law works in our lives. It is the knowing that we are unconditionally loved by an unconditionally loving and merciful God. He knows us through and through and sees our true, authentic selves. John 10:10 reads: "I come so that they may have life and have it more abundantly."

God created the law of attraction.

■ ■ ■

The word *conscious* is defined as "to be aware." The basic idea of conscious language is to be aware of what you are thinking and saying. It is about using your language to claim or connect with what you actually choose to have.

> ## To be conscious *is* to be aware.
>
> ■ ■ ■

Conscious language requires a heightened awareness and is a vital step to being the playful and powerful Warrior that you are. Your conscious language awareness will strengthen your understanding of the power of your words, allowing you to experience the changes in your body when you speak in a way that honors the fullness of your whole self. Consciously chosen thoughts and words will transform your circumstances and support your actions and the creation of the life you choose.

One believes whatever one repeats to one's self, whether the statement be true or false. If a man repeats a lie over and over, he will eventually accept the lie as truth. Moreover, he will *believe* it to be the truth. Every man is what he is because of the dominating thoughts he permits to occupy his mind.

The thoughts that you deliberately place in your mind and the words you use shape your experiences just as a computer operating system instructs a computer. Your thoughts, feelings, emotions, and words form your human operating system. This determines your reality. Just as one change in a line of software code changes an entire program, your alteration of even one word will change your entire experience of a specific situation.

All thoughts and words have meaning. All words you speak are extremely important, and every word has meaning to the subconscious mind. That is what conscious language is. It is understanding this powerful technique, or system, that will assist you to be more aware of your words. You will also start to use more effective language choices for yourself.

Learning and understanding conscious language will show you how:

- To speak "what is."
- The words you speak are self-fulfilling prophecies.
- The words you speak with feeling and specificity equals manifestation.
- Your subconscious mind translates your language literally and does exactly what you tell it to do.
- To identify and upgrade your internal dialogue and transform it quickly into success at home, at work, and at play.
- To awaken your internal guidance system, listen to your true, authentic self, and let it be your guide.
- To use language to positively upgrade your self-esteem, health, finances, family life, and any other area where you use language to produce results.
- Being fully and completely present in your speaking (internal voice and external voice) is essential to success.
- To choose or modify your "first words." The first thoughts and words that come to you are important keys to upgrading your life. What are you thinking or saying first?
- To communicate in first person. Communicate using "I" statements (eliminating "you" or "they").
- To become your own optimal self-programmer, easily removing and upgrading your thoughts and words into success in your own operating system.
- To become your own conscious partner with your life, health, and prosperity.
- To coach yourself into success again and again and again.

Conscious language affects every one of the Warrior principles, steps, skills, and life actions. Your language is one of the easiest ways to determine whether what you desire is a match for what you believe you are able to have.

In many instances, language exerts a profound influence without your even being conscious of it. Being aware of, being conscious of, or being present with the words you use will help you harness the powers of your language. This will also maximize your choices of attaining extraordinary life, health, and prosperity.

Conscious language is a system of language designed to find your limiting beliefs and rewrite them into your highest magnificent choices. Conscious language, the words you place into the world, provides instructions to your subconscious mind and to the universe. People often say things that are self-limiting or self-negating. Statements about yourself mirror your personal power. Speak positively and speak to what *"is"* versus what *"is not."*

At first this subject may require some time and practice to fully understand. When you start understanding and using what you learn about your conscious language, you will have a heightened awareness and you will start to see positive actions for yourself. Your words will create the life you deserve and choose to have.

There are many daily actions to choose and responsibilities to fulfill. The very thought of monitoring your words may seem like a luxury. You might think time is too limited for you to fully engage in conscious language and that your good intentions should be enough.

> ## Statements about yourself mirror your personal power.
> ■ ■ ■

What you think of, speak about, and act upon creates your reality. First you think of something. You get an idea. Then you speak about it. You act upon your thoughts by placing your language into the universe. Then you express your thoughts and words, and you move your desires forward. Each one of these steps is critical to the actualization of your desire. Each step, when performed in a positive way, will result in a positive final product or result.

All of the negative and positive thoughts and language you have previously placed into the universe are still in process and motion for you. You may have previously used countless sabotaging words and statements that created unwanted results for you. Unless you cancel these previous thoughts and language, you may still see the results of what you already created for yourself, both negative and positive.

Your conscious language is constant. Implementing positive conscious language may require some time for the positive process to have the impact you will eventually receive. In doing so, you will open up a whole new world for yourself. You are a powerful creator with the ability to create what you desire. Use the law God has given you and choose to use positive thoughts, words, and action statements. You will immediately begin the positive process of living how you choose to live for yourself. The Warrior you.

Are you ready to be completely aware of your thoughts, words, language, and actions?

■ ■ ■

WARRIOR ACTION STEPS

■ ■ ■

CONSCIOUS LANGUAGE: MANIFEST YOUR TRUE DESIRES

Every word has meaning to the subconscious mind.

1. Choose to look at *yourself* as a POWERFUL creator.

2. Are you ready to choose the shift in your conscious language? Reflect on the words you have spoken that have created self-fulfilling prophecies for you. Did you receive what you desired? Say what you choose to have and *what is* versus *what is not.*

3. Create awareness of your thoughts and words. Be aware of all the thoughts and words you speak with feeling and specificity. Eliminate self-sabotaging and negative thoughts, words, and statements. Use positive words to create and to receive.

4. Identify and upgrade your internal dialogue. Quickly transform your internal dialogue into what you choose to have at home, work, and play.

5. Awaken your internal guidance system, and listen to your authentic self. Let it be your guide. Remember, you have the power to choose again. Choose to think and speak in a self-accomplishing manner, and it will increase your success.

■ ■ ■

Be Bold, Be Playful, Be Powerful, and Enjoy Your Great Warrior Adventure!

CHAPTER ELEVEN

■ ■ ■

Conscious Language: The Power of Your Thoughts

Warriors understand their thoughts create manifestation.

■ ■ ■

"As a man thinketh, so he is." "Man is created by thought; what a man thinks upon, that he becomes." Thought is a dynamic force. Thought moves. Thought creates. You are able to work wonders with the power of thought. Through the instrumentality of thought, you acquire creative power—hence the power of positive thinking.

Your mind assumes the form of anything it contemplates. When you think of an object, your mind shapes itself into the form of that object. When you change your thought, your mind also changes its shape. Many modifications continually arise in the mind. Your thoughts rapidly change. Your mind also changes its shape rapidly. Every moment, your mind is continually creating hundreds of these thought forms and continually dispersing them again.

Think you are strong; strong you become. Think you are weak; then weak you become. Think you are a fool; foolish you become. A Warrior forms his own character, becoming that which he thinks. When you focus on courage, you shall work courage into your character. When you think honorably, you shall gradually create for yourself an honorable character.

Steady, persevering thoughts set up a definite habit of the mind, and that habit manifests itself as a quality in the character. The thread of thought is woven into mental and moral qualities. These qualities in their totality form your character. You are able to build your character as surely as a mason is able to build a wall. The first step towards a deliberate creation of character lies then in the deliberate choosing of what you will think and then of thinking persistently on the quality chosen.

Thought is a vital living force. Thought is the most vital, subtle, and powerful force that exists in the universe. Every change in thought is accompanied by a vibration of its mental matter. Every thought creates a biochemical response in your body. These reactions vary from negligible to intense. Science has known this for some time. When you think about food, your saliva glands may be stimulated. When you think of the person that irritates you most, your body constricts and tenses up. When you reflect upon your most fulfilling moments, endorphins are released in your body and you feel more relaxed and at peace. Every memory, whether positive or negative, elicits an internal physical response. With every thought, there is a biochemical response in your body.

Thought is a living force.

■ ■ ■

The impact of a thought on your nervous system ranges in intensity according to the level of emotion associated with your thought. For example, reflecting on the death of a loved one creates a much deeper emotional response than remembering to buy food or noticing that you stepped on an insect. The more intense the emotion, the greater the impact the thought has on the physical body.

The quickest way to evaluate this for yourself is to choose to notice the emotions you experience repeatedly. These are the emotions your body has grown accustomed to experiencing and unconsciously works to elicit.

Anger, stress, anxiety, fear, depression, sadness, frustration, guilt, and worry may be a few of the emotional thought patterns to investigate more closely. Behind every emotion is a thought or set of thoughts. If stress is a common pattern in your life, you may have thoughts such as, "This must be accomplished before I am able to relax." "I have too much to do." "I can't get it all done." If depression is something you experience, something as basic as "I feel depressed" may be the thought feeding the emotion. You may have one or multiple thoughts feeding this pattern.

When you have a fearful image in your mind, that image can seem so powerful that your body may physically react in a fearful way. You may break out in a sweat or begin to tremble. Your heart rate may also rise, along with your blood pressure. Your body is unable to decipher the difference between an image held in your mind and an actual event. The pictures you maintain in your mind and project outward, then become your reality.

Your dominant thoughts and self-concepts are expressed verbally in language and become the "videos" you play in your head. These videos begin running as soon as you are faced with a critical situation. These thoughts will be played back to you and determine whether you act in a positive or negative manner.

Whether it is a goal, dream, or aspiration, a project or an idea, your health or your body, a solution to a challenge or a brand new endeavor, a clear and vivid image will form in your mind and use conscious language to speed you toward it. The more crystallized your instructions to your subconscious mind and the universe, the faster the universe will help you bring your plan into reality.

You may also experience a variety of positive or empowering emotions. Joy, happiness, peace, excitement, pleasure, and playfulness are a few. Investigating the thoughts associated with empowering emotions is useful because you are able to learn to strengthen and intensify these. These will provide more fulfillment and connection. How conscious are you of the thoughts and emotional patterns that are running your life? What thoughts and emotions are you constantly creating for yourself?

Warriors understand that thought is the first step toward action.

■ ■ ■

Seven Keys to Transforming Your Thoughts

Since your thoughts shape your reality, start focusing on thoughts that feel good and perpetuate success and happiness in your life. Below are seven keys to transforming your thoughts for what *you choose to have.*

1. **Be aware** – Before you are able to influence your thoughts, you must become aware of them. How else do you know there is a disempowering thought lurking in your mind? Your emotions serve as signals to catch your attention. These feelings may be subtle or extreme.

A feeling that something is off creates discomfort, anxiety, or a mild sense of resistance or depression and is worth paying attention to. Some reactions are blatant and obvious, serving as giant clues the mind has attached to a thought. Become a detective and identify the thought or thoughts that are associated with the feeling. Awareness is the first key. You are able to shift what you are aware of.

2. **Determine it is true in reality** – So often, the thoughts that drive your feelings have zero basis in reality because they are untrue. You become attached to thoughts that are simply fantasy. When an event happens, your mind instantaneously attaches a meaning (*meaning* is a synonym for *thought*) to the

occurrence. It is important to recognize the myriad ways that you may distort reality.

You exaggerate or minimize it. You deny it. You think it should be different than it is. You defend it. You argue with it. You forecast it. Each of these results in creating chaos, stress, or anxiety in your life. Separating the facts of what happened from the meaning or interpretation is one way to connect to your true and actual reality.

3. Identify the impact – Oftentimes, a thought you investigate appears to be factual or true; however, the resulting feeling is one of stress, anxiety, or sadness. When a thought is true and you find that the result is different than what you choose to have, identify the impact. Analyze the impact and identify what you choose to change to receive the result you choose to have. When you continue to attach to this thought, how will it make you feel? How will you treat others? How will you live your life if you constantly focus on this thought?

4. Be willing – For any transformation to occur, you must be willing to choose a shift. You may know you have an addiction to food, drugs, sex, TV, or alcohol, and without a genuine willingness to choose a shift, nothing will disrupt the destructive behavior. Such is the case with the thoughts you are consciously or unconsciously are addicted to. This *authentic willingness* to choose a shift in thinking creates profound positive actions for you.

5. Just let go – When you have negative thoughts, simply let them go. Then focus on the positive opposite thought. Drive away from your mind all unnecessary, useless, and obnoxious thoughts. Useless thoughts impede your growth; obnoxious thoughts are stumbling blocks to your advancement. Honor yourself by entertaining thoughts that are helpful and useful. Eliminate the "old grooves" and habits. Be on careful watch of your thoughts, and eliminate or just let go of all negative ones.

6. Redirect focus – Animals focus on whatever you place in front of them. The mind works very much the same way and becomes the focus of its reality. When caught up in addictive thoughts,

consciously redirect your focus on something more positive or neutral. If your spouse is running late, embrace the beauty in your environment. When you find yourself frustrated in traffic, focus on your breathing, the music in the car, or the opportunity to relax and slow down. Your thought is a powerful means of redirecting your focus. Consider shifting your internal dialog. Choose words that will empower you over words that deplete your energy.

7. **Replace it** – Eliminate and replace all negative thoughts with something more empowering. Consciously choosing the opposite of the original thought and replacing it with a positive thought is a simple solution.

Be wise and be conscious with your thoughts.

■ ■ ■

Another way to find a replacement is to turn the statement around. Identify a thought that is "as true" or "truer" and more positive than the original statement. Simply align more with what you choose to create or attract into your life.

Thoughts lead to action. Thoughts are the sources of all actions. Thinking is the real action. A Warrior watches his thoughts and eliminates all negative thoughts as they arise from the surface of his mind.

You have control over your thoughts, and you are able to create immense positive power with intense concentration. Focus on positive thoughts and allow your Warrior self to create and shape your words.

How conscious are you in choosing your thoughts?

■ ■ ■

WARRIOR ACTION STEPS

■ ■ ■

CONSCIOUS LANGUAGE: THE POWER OF YOUR THOUGHTS

What you focus on is what you receive. Thought is the power that produces tangible riches from formless substance.

1. Remember to look at yourself as a POWERFUL creator.

2. Thought is a vital living force. How conscious are you of the thoughts and emotional patterns that are running your life? What thoughts and emotions are you constantly creating for yourself? Are you open to always being conscious of your thoughts? Are they positive or negative?

    a. Name three common thoughts you have.

    b. What thoughts and emotions are you constantly creating for yourself? Name three of them.

    c. Eliminate self-sabotaging and negative thoughts and insert positive uplifting thoughts. Name three negative thoughts you consistently have, and list what their positive counterpart is.

    d. Redirect focus. When caught up in addictive thoughts, consciously redirect your focus on something more positive or neutral.

    e. Eliminate and replace all negative thoughts with something more empowering.

■ ■ ■

Be Bold, Be Playful, Be Powerful, and Enjoy Your Great Warrior Adventure!

CHAPTER TWELVE

■   ■   ■

Conscious Language: The Power of Your Words

Do you realize that every spoken word creates your reality?

■ ■ ■

Warriors understand the power of their words. The specific words you use reveals internal experiences and shapes external realities. With conscious use of your language, you will create word choices that heal rather than hurt, build rather than destroy, live rather than die, and create the results you truly desire rather than those you fear. Sometimes all it requires is the shift of a few words to change your whole world. Are you ready to choose the shift in your conscious language?

The words you think and say are a program or habit you have created. They may be limiting and stunting your very own growth and the outcome of your true desires. In other words, you are stopping you from becoming your higher self, the best you are and will be, and from enjoying your life to the fullest.

In the past, you have spoken unconsciously, creating experiences and situations in your life. Many of these spoken words have created outcomes that are undesirable for yourself. By learning and understanding conscious language, you will experience exactly how self-sabotaging words and phrases have been operating in your life and in your world.

Focus on what you *choose to have* versus what you do not want. Say what is versus what is not. Did you know that each time you say "I want" or "I need," you are focusing on a lack of what you have or what you do not want? When you say "I want," you are in effect saying, "I don't have this." It means desire without having. "I need" works the same way; it means, "This is *not* in my current or present life." Lack! Lack! Lack! Is more lack what you desire to have?

If you say, "I want help," you are saying "I desire help without having it" or "I lack help." The word *want* means "lack." With conscious awareness, you are able to upgrade to "I choose help" or "I will find help" or "I give myself help" or "Please help me."

If you are unable to currently experience the life, health, or prosperity you desire, it is most likely because of the words you use to create less of it instead of more of it. Instead of saying "I want" or "I need," substitute the following positive choice of words: Change the want or need to *choose*. I *choose* to create.

Read this statement: "I want to meet my soul mate." This is a perfect example of how choosing your words will either empower your results or hinder them. All words have energetic charges to them. By using the word *want* in your declaration, you are putting out an energy that is limiting. Now consider this: "I choose to meet my soul mate." Or "I have found my soul mate." Both have a much greater, cleaner, and more powerful energy to them.

By expressing your desire in terms of what you want, you are actually creating more of the wanting than anything else. When you are doing the choosing, then you are empowering yourself with the choices you have chosen.

When you say, "I'm sorry," you are actually saying who you are is a sorry human being. The same goes for "I'm sick," "I'm tired,"

"I'm stupid," and "I'm dying. You get the idea. All of these statements are creating more of what you are saying when you say them. Is this what you truly desire to have? Replace the words as follows:

> "I'm sorry" with "I apologize."
> "I'm sick" with "I am healthy."
> "I'm tired" with "I'm rested" or "I have energy."
> "I'm stupid" with "I'm smart."
> "I'm dying" or "That is to die for" or "You're killing me" with "I'm living" or "That is to live for" or "I love that."

See how easy it is to change your "I" statements from having a negative meaning to a positive meaning? When you eliminate the words "I'm sorry" from your vocabulary, you will increase your self-esteem immediately. When you eliminate the words "I'm sick," you will feel much more healthy. When you eliminate the words "I'm tired," will have more energy. When you eliminate the words "I'm stupid," you will feel brighter and smarter, and you will increase your self-esteem immediately. When you eliminate the words "I am dying" with "I am living," you will create more life. By choosing these simple changes in language, you will feel better, be healthier, and enjoy living more. Your life, health, and prosperity will increase.

When something is exactly and specifically spoken, it is exactly and specifically created. If you could sit in a doctor's office and listen to patients describe their physical challenges, you would hear them describing, unconsciously, their states. The word *dis-ease* means "lack of ease or trouble." Those patients would be actually decreeing that they are sick and full of trouble. They would also be creating those diseases or ailments for themselves. Instead of stating what they are "desiring to heal," they are actually creating "sickness." They are feeding what they actually do *not* desire versus what they *do* desire. Sickness is a consciousness; that is, it is consciously being fed by their own thoughts and words.

> ## The power to change your
> ## world lies in your words.
>
> ■ ■ ■

Another commonly used word is the word *not*. The definition of *not* is "to express negation, denial, refusal, or prohibition; interjection to indicate that a previous statement is untrue."

Instead of stating what you *do not* desire to have, state what you *do* desire to have, and what is. A good example would be if you are feeling unhealthy, state what is and state the following: "I am healthy." The healing begins to happen. It starts the manifestation of "I am healthy." Imagine already being and feeling healthy. Your subconscious will believe you are feeling healthy and start sending the positive signals/energy through your body. This will assist in the healing process.

When you say "I can't," "I don't," "It is hard," "But," " I shouldn't," "I've got to," "I wish," "I won't," "I can't afford it," "It is a problem," "That's too complicated," and so forth, you are actually matching, creating, and synchronizing with events that you choose to have happen. You are giving your personal power away to these events. These are self-sabotaging statements. They are affecting your life, health, prosperity, passions, emotions, heart's desires, goals, dreams, and aspirations. Make sure you incorporate positive thoughts, words, and statements to manifest what you do desire.

Another commonly used word is *try*. When you say you are going to "try" to do something, the implication that it is *not* for sure. Somewhere in there it implies that failure is possible. It is because unconsciously, you are hesitant to truly desire or plan to accomplish your task, goal, objective, or process. By using *try,* you are unwittingly setting yourself up for failure. You are acknowledging beforehand that you may avoid achieving the task, goal, objective, or process. In short, the word *try* provides you with a handy excuse for failure.

Why use the word *try* at all? Saying "I will," "I will do it," or "I will do my best to get there" provides a whole other feeling to what you are conveying. "Will," "do," or "doing" involves completing a task, goal, objective, or process. An interesting and often overlooked part of all this is the ability to avoid words that are negating a negative statement. What the heck do I mean by this?

But is another word commonly used to create a negative. The definition of *but* is "on the contrary; yet; except; save; unless; if not; except that; without the circumstance that; otherwise than." The word *but* cancels out what was just stated previously.

In most cases, the word *but* is creating separatism or canceling out what was previously said. An example is, "He is a great leader, but more than that, he is also trustworthy." The word *but* cancels out the first part of that particular statement. What is being said, is that success is unavailable to everyone. The word *but* negates anything that is said before it.

What would be empowering and inclusive is using the word *and*. The word *and* is inclusive whereas *but* creates separatism or cancels out. Here is the same statement using *and*. "He is a strong leader, and more than that, he is also trustworthy." This statement creates inclusion. Any time you use the word *but*, exchange it with the word *and*. Your statements will have much more positive flow and power.

A word such as *limitless* is actually drawing the subconscious mind to focus on limits. Are limits what you choose to have? When you say something such as "having limitless abundance," limitless is placing limits on the abundance. Rephrase the statement to say what you actually do desire for yourself: "There is great abundance." or "I have great abundance."

Here's another example of negating a negative statement: "Having a wonderful relationship is easy, effortless, and fun." This is actually drawing "effort" into your life. Eliminating the word *effortless* and saying only "easy and fun" makes everything shift to "easy and fun." Relationships are easy and fun.

Do you see how common phrases are used to be positive and actually have a negative meaning or action? How many words do you use that creates negativity or even destroys your desires?

Focus on what you choose to have.
■ ■ ■

The use of negative fun—making fun of, jesting, or using sarcasm—goes into the subconscious mind on some level. The word *sarcasm* comes from a word that means "the tearing of flesh." Sarcasm is received directly by the subconscious mind. Even when the mental body knows one is joking, the emotional body feels pain or hurt.

There is a way to laugh in beauty, in joy, and in harmony with our greater truth. Laughing with yourself, or lightening up, is really important. Joking around is a great form of expression. Make sure you are being positive when doing so. This honors both you and the ones you are joking around with. Be positive and use humor to build self-esteem.

Understand the law of focus. Another very important aspect of conscious language is the law of focus. *Whatever you place your attention on is what you create.* It is important to focus on the positive thing you desire rather than the negative thing you choose to avoid.

When you say, "I am not aging," you are actually focusing on aging. This ensures that you are and will actually age more quickly. Instead focus on being healthy, vibrant, youthful, and young.

Review your own statements and affirmations and the words you say out loud or to yourself to see how positive you are actually being. Identifying when you are using words and phrases that are self-sabotaging will make it easier for you to become aware of them and to quickly upgrade your language. Upgrading your conscious language will have an immediate, profound, and positive influence in your life.

Upgrading your language is a rebooting of your own greatness, perfection, power, and magnificence. Upgrading your language turns your greatest weakness into your greatest strength. Choice is always available to you, and you always have the ability to re-choose. Upgrading also aligns your authentic self with your choices in life while providing, purpose, positive intention, passion, energy, conviction, focus, ingenuity, resilience, fulfillment, and results. Being fully present in your current reality is your access point for shifting it with your language. It creates a commitment to listening to yourself and to others and creates empowering action for you.

A conscious language Warrior is practiced at hearing and listening to the mechanics of both their own language and that of others. They are able to hear the questions, uncertainties, and disconnections in how you use language and ask your own questions back to you, helping you become conscious of your internal dialogue, beliefs, thought patterns, and positive word power.

Use your positive word power. Conscious language exists within every conversation someone is willing to have about himself. It is a system of language used to hear the limiting patterns, programmed beliefs, and thoughts that form within statements a person is willing to make about themselves ("I" statements). Your beliefs and thoughts form your patterning, and they are projected visually, much like a hologram. Every word you say is a demand to your universe and defines your reality as it sets the requirement for what your future will hold.

Increase your positive word power by focusing on positive, healthy, and living "I" statements. Each and every statement may be restated into a positive and creative form to truly attract what you desire to have.

> **Success for you is predictable and attainable with your thoughts, words, and actions.**
>
> ■ ■ ■

There are three dynamics that happen when you use "I choose." First, you provide empowerment to yourself. Second, you decide to make the choice for yourself. And third, you come from a position of strength instead of a position of weakness. You decide to choose, which creates your personal choice. When you choose, you are using your power to do so. Always come from your positive position of strength.

The best positive reinforcement for conscious language statements and affirmations are any statements that start with the words "I am" and "I am and I choose." These are the most powerful statements you are able to say to connect yourself to the source of "all that is." Whatever you follow up with after "I am," make sure it is a positive word or statement for you. Always come from your positive strength.

Two of the most powerful words in the English language are the words *I* and *am*. These two words tell every part of you—your personality, your subconscious, your ego, and your spirit—exactly who you are. "I am" defines who you are.

When you use the phrase "I am," your subconscious mind instantly goes on alert. You are providing the universe and your own mind with a road map for what you desire, have, or choose to become.

Using the phrase "I am" with negative or limiting words, such as "tired," "poor," or "angry," will enable them to become self-fulfilling prophecies. A more positive use of "I am" in your conscious language would be saying this statement in a positive and powerful manner. Use "I am" statements for manifestation of the results you choose to have happen in your life.

Warriors say, "I have energy. I am wealthy. I have and am loved. I am at peace. I am powerful. I am capable. I am patient. I am healthy. I am ready. I am positive." Always come from your positive position of strength. When saying "I am," use words and actions you choose to create. Start by using and choosing statements with positive words, actions, desires, and choices, and see what changes start to happen in your life. Speak these statements with feeling, and watch how quickly what you choose will manifest in your life.

Cleaning up your language to speak consciously will require practice on your part. It is a way to immediately upgrade your life. You will be able to overcome the negative voices of others—or even your own inner self—and turn your language into positive reality. You will also be able to understand and avoid using words that will tear you down and tell you that you are unable to succeed. You are able to choose what you desire to be and do.

Choose time to get into this habit of choosing your words wisely. Being able to express yourself in clear, positive ways will communicate something very powerful to your subconscious mind and to your listeners. Even when things are challenging, find ways to express what you are going through in such a way that allow for the possibilities of empowerment and solutions to show up. *You are a powerful Warrior creator.*

> **Use "I am" statements for manifestation of the results you choose to have happen in your life.**
>
> ■ ■ ■

Below is a list of common communicative words that are part of everyday conscious language and that create either negative or positive actions. Become familiar with both the negative and positive words and their effects.

Positive Word Choices	Negative Word Choices
I am	I need
I choose	I can't
I have	I might
And	But
I enjoy	If
I give myself permission to	It's hard
What I am learning is	Try
I understand	Attempt
I can	Kinda
I will	Working on
I am able to	I've got to
I empower	I should
I claim	I wish they would
I accept	I don't know
I know	I'm not good enough
I love	I can't afford
My outcome	It's a problem
My power	I didn't do it
I am clear	It's not my fault
Is	That's the way it's always been done
Are	That's too complicated
	I don't have the resources available
	That will never work
	There's not enough time
	I think
	I am stuck
	I'll give it my best shot
	Hopefully
	Someday
	Maybe
	Not

When you catch yourself using words with negative connotations or ones that indicate a weakened or loss of responsibility for your actions or choices, say something such as "cancel," "clear," "delete," or "my choice is." Replace the words with a positive or empowering conscious choice of words. This allows you to cancel out any self-sabotaging or negative thoughts, words, and statements you may have thought or said.

An example of using these statements is, "I have created limitless abundance for myself." Because you used the word "limitless," you are creating limits for yourself. Choose to say something such as, "cancel" or "clear." Now restate your thought: "I have great abundance in my life." You have just canceled any limits regarding what you said and created a powerful and unlimiting statement for yourself. You have the power to choose what you do desire for yourself. As a reminder, always come from your positive position of strength.

We are all accustomed to speaking and hearing people use language in negative or limiting ways. Being precise in the words you speak will begin to pay off. By actively choosing words that reflect positive responsibility for your choices, your life will begin to change. The good news is that with awareness and monitoring, you will develop a powerful new habit.

Warriors communicate best when they are clear about who they are and what they intend. When you are talking to someone, ask yourself this question: "Who am I being, and what is the impact of my words on myself and the people around me?" The power of your words lies in the intention behind them.

Harness your word power to work for you. Many people choose words that work against them. Select words that create a visual of your desired outcome, and choose each word because it matters. Choose to have better results by checking your words. Warriors know their intent and create it by their own thoughts, words, and actions.

WARRIOR ACTION STEPS

■ ■ ■

CONSCIOUS LANGUAGE: THE POWER OF YOUR WORDS

Choose your words wisely and with care.

1. Words create images in your mind, and these images change the outer events of your world. Images provide you with vivid desire and energy.

2. Remember to look at yourself as a powerful creator. Increase your positive word power by focusing on positive, healthy, and living "I" statements. Start using and saying "I" statements—"I am [a positive statement]."

3. Create awareness of your words and start using positive actions and empowering words such as "I am," "I choose," "I have," "I enjoy," "I give myself permission to," "I choose to make it easy," "What I'm learning is," "I can," "I will," "I empower," "I claim," "I Accept," "I know," "I love," "My outcome," and "My power."

4. Eliminate self-sabotaging and negative words and statements such as "try," "but," "want," "need," "can't," "if," "hard," "problem," and so forth. Remember, you have the power to choose again.

5. When listening to someone talk negatively or in a limiting language, rephrase what is being said in conscious language. Even though it may be obvious to the person what you're doing, he or she will get the message of how negative the words sound. More importantly, you will be caring for yourself and developing a powerful new habit. When you are experiencing negative communication, begin a sentence using "imagine" or "interesting." These words set up the mind to look for creativity, which is the key to finding solutions.

6. Decipher seemingly harmless sayings that are rooted in limiting beliefs. The best way to be aware of and to realize the use of your language is simply to go to your feelings. Ask yourself, "Does this make me feel good?" or "Why am I feeling this?" or "What does this mean?" Your feelings are powerful guides for steering you in the right direction. Pay attention to them.

7. The specific words you use reveals internal experiences and shapes external realities. Create the results you truly desire and focus on saying what is and what you *choose to have.*

■ ■ ■

Be Bold, Be Playful, Be Powerful, and Enjoy Your Great Warrior Adventure!

CHAPTER THIRTEEN

■ ■ ■

Your Warrior Stage

Warriors know and understand when to get on someone else's stage

■ ■ ■

I finally came to realize that the more I chose to assist some of the closest people in my life, the more I found tension and conflict with them. I had good intentions to help them, and many times my help simply created a negative situation. I was totally confused as to why this was the case because my intentions to help were pure. Have you ever had painful experiences such as chaos, anger, frustration, or resentment for simply choosing to help someone you care about?

Were you surprised by his or her reaction when all you were doing was helping? Did he or she fire back at you, and then you fired right back? Were you asked by the other person to assist or help?

Most of us have experienced such situations. In most cases, we had great intentions, especially if the person is one of our loved ones. Most of these past negative experiences of chaos, anger, frustration, and resentment are typically with loved ones and the people we care about most. Isn't it ironic? Even with great intentions, we may create unnecessary pain for ourselves.

My friend Greg Klein shared the following example with me. I immediately saw the light on how I had and was creating some of my own pain simply by jumping on and being on someone else's stage.

Have you ever seen a comic perform at a comedy show or on television? Visualize the following:

Stage #1 Scenario – Jumping on Someone's Stage

A comic is performing his monologue. He is simply rolling along enjoying his performance and the audience's reaction to the performance. Everyone is happy with the way the show is progressing.

All of a sudden, midway through the performance, a man in the front row starts to heckle the comic. At first the comic ignores the heckler. A few minutes later, however, the heckler interrupts the comic again. Now the comic is upset. The audience is upset because the heckler is disrupting the show.

Then the comic fires back at the heckler. The audience becomes angrier—the patrons paid to see the comic perform. The audience yells at the heckler to shut up and sit down.

The heckler ignores the audience and jumps onto the stage. The comic is now face to face with the heckler. A fight is imminent. The comic and the heckler both want to go at it. The audience wants to knock out the heckler. Everyone is upset, and all of the drama has caused everyone to lose sight of what the purpose of being there was.

Stage #2 Scenario – Being Invited onto a Stage

A comic is performing his monologue. He is simply rolling along. He is enjoying his performance. The audience is enjoying the performance. Everybody is happy with the way the show is progressing.

All of a sudden, midway through the performance, the comic stops and asks, "Do I have anyone here who would like to participate in the next part of my show?" A man in the front row raises his hand. The comic asks the man to join him on stage. The man stands up, runs over to the stage, and jumps on it. He is smiling from ear to ear.

The comic says, "Let's give a round of applause for our volunteer." Everyone is clapping and cheering. The man is now beaming. The audience is happy, the man is happy, and the comic is happy.

The comic performs his skit with the man. Everyone enjoys it. Upon completion of the skit, the comic thanks the man and the man thanks the comic. There is applause from the audience. Everyone leaves happy.

> **Remember, you have the power to choose to be on someone's stage. Even if you are invited, it is *your* choice.**
>
> ■ ■ ■

Stage #3 Scenario – Keeping Your Stage Clean

Imagine having the exact same stage above. This time there is no show going on. The lights are on and the stage is clean. You desire to have a clean stage ready for the next performance. This is your stage and you are responsible for it.

Everything is set for the next performance when, all of a sudden, a man barges in and jumps onto your stage uninvited. He is attempting to take over your stage. What are you going to do? How are you going to respond?

What are you able to learn from these examples? In the first example, everyone became very upset because someone jumped on the comic's stage uninvited. Have you ever jumped on someone else's stage? Did you have good intentions and ended up having a similar action as to what happened on Stage #1?

In the second example, everyone was happy because someone was invited onto the stage. Have you ever been invited onto someone else's stage? Have you had a similar experience as to what happened on Stage #2?

In the third example, you have a pristine stage. Then, all of a sudden, someone jumps onto your stage uninvited. This has most likely happened to you before and will most likely happen again. The key is to know people are going to attempt to jump onto your stage. By having this knowledge and understanding, you will be able to decide how to respond positively. How are you going to respond when this happens?

There will come a time when you may desire to invite someone onto your stage. When you offer the invitation, make sure you are open to receiving that person's message.

People jump on our stage uninvited just as we jump on other people's stages uninvited. Any time this happens, we risk having conflict and drama.

When you are invited onto someone's stage, the other person is *asking* for your assistance. A key question to ask yourself is: "Do I choose to be on this person's stage?" Remember, you have the choice whether to be on that person's stage, even if you are invited. It is *your* choice.

Look at some of the conflict or drama in your life and there is a high probability there is someone on someone else's stage— uninvited. The only time you should ever get on someone else's stage is when you are invited. Then make sure it serves and honors you.

> ## The best time to step onto someone else's stage is when you are invited.
>
> ■ ■ ■

Remember, when you are invited onto someone else's stage, be sure to honor what is best for you before you decide to go onto his or her stage. Always make sure getting onto someone else's stage serves you, or you will be setting yourself up for your own frustration, drama, and discomfort. Saying "no" to the invitation to be onto someone else's stage simply means you are honoring what is best for you. Honor your Warrior stage first.

The next time you feel the desire to jump onto someone else's stage, what are you going to do?

■ ■ ■

WARRIOR ACTION STEPS

■ ■ ■

YOUR WARRIOR STAGE

Be connected to yourself. When you change the way you look at things, the things you look at change. —Wayne W. Dyer

1. Honor your Warrior stage.

2. The best time to step onto someone else's stage is when you are invited. When invited, make sure it serves and honors you. Identify three times when you have jumped onto someone else's stage uninvited. What was the result? Did it serve you and honor you?

3. When feeling the desire to be on someone else's stage, always ask the other person first for permission.

4. Identify three times when you have had someone jump onto your Warrior stage uninvited. What was the result?

5. When you invite someone onto your stage, make sure you are open to receiving that person's message.

■ ■ ■

Be Bold, Be Playful, Be Powerful, and Enjoy Your Great Warrior Adventure!

CHAPTER FOURTEEN

■ ■ ■

Your Warrior Greatness. Always Come from Your Best

Success is peace of mind that can be obtained from the self-satisfaction of knowing that I have made the effort to do the very best of which I am capable. —COACH JOHN WOODEN

■ ■ ■

The first Webster's dictionary ever printed in 1806 gave the description of success as "fortunate, happy, kind, and prosperous." Notice that in this definition, fame, fortune, and power have no part of success.

Coach John Wooden's definition of success (noted above) parallels that of the 1806 definition. Success is peace of mind, which is the direct result of self-satisfaction in knowing you did your best to become the best that you are capable of becoming.

I am a big sports fan. I have been a player, coach, and viewer. I have read countless books, magazines, and articles on sports. I also enjoy reading and sharing stories of great triumphs in athletics. I view athletes the same as I view Warriors. The same principles apply to both athletes and Warriors. With that said, here are a few examples of great coaches and players who have performed as Warriors both on and off the field or court of play. They embraced their Warrior greatness, and their stories have had an impact upon me. They have also shown, regardless of the challenges, they were able to look within and be the Warriors they are.

At the beginning of the 1972–1973 basketball season, Coach Dale Brown's LSU team was predicted to have another losing season (they had finished the previous season at 10–16 and ended up dead last in the SEC). It was obvious from the start of the season that this team had very little perceived talent, especially compared to the rest of the SEC teams. Coach Brown knew he had to do something to make up for their shortcomings in talent.

Coach Brown made up for their shortcomings with simplicity and constant repetition, a lot of hard work, and great conditioning. He knew if they were conditioned to their best ability, they would outwork, outplay, and outhustle other teams. In fact, this team was known as "The Hustlers." A Knoxville newspaper reporter wrote an article on Coach Brown's team and recommended giving the LSU players saliva tests because they played like super human beings.

LSU shocked more than a few people that year. They defeated the number two team in the country. They finished 14–10 overall and 9–9 in league play. Coach Brown won the SEC Coach of the Year award.

When I was a young boy, this was proof to me that if I worked to the best of my abilities, practiced hard, and hustled, I would be happy with the results for myself. This has proven to be true in my adult life as well. Are you getting after it, hustling and giving your very best to be your best?

What's so revolutionary about the idea of choosing the effort to do your best? Coach Wooden focused on his effort to do his best. He chose to compete within himself and translated this concept to his teams. Even after winning consecutive national championships,

Coach Wooden chose more. He asked his teams to play *their best* each and every game.

Coach Wooden began every season by talking about the competition. He told his players to focus on what they controlled: their thoughts, words, and actions. He said when they played their best, they would be successful. When they chose to play without playing their best, then they would never be successful, no matter how many games they won.

Coach Wooden believed in teaching his players to put every ounce of effort they had even into the most mundane tasks. He had his players start the season by learning how to put on their socks and shoes. Yes, how to put on socks and shoes. The importance of this was to ensure every detail of playing basketball was practiced and perfected.

The celebrated Green Bay Packers coach, Vince Lombardi, shared the same view. Focus on being *your* best. His teams spent hours upon hours focusing on the fundamentals. He knew by practicing the simple tasks over and over, his players would respond to their best in execution.

Coaches Wooden, Brown, and Lombardi had their teams practice over and over on every single detail until their teams were performing at their very best. It was this effort they were looking for. That was the reason to compete—to make the effort to be your best. To utilize the most of the talent God has given you. To choose the effort to become the best human being possible. These coaches taught—and proved—that when you choose that effort, winning will happen.

> **The only person in the whole wide world who knows how much effort you applied and whether you truly did your best is you.**
>
> ■　■　■

Here are several more stories of Warriors who have inspired me. They all faced the choice to give up or choose to reach inside and decide and to be the best they could be. Many know the story of Michael Jordan, considered to be one of the greatest basketball players of all time. In fact, only a year after joining the team, as a tenth grader, he was cut from the varsity team. This only pushed him to work harder at perfecting his game. As he later said, "I think that not making the varsity team drove me to really work at my game, and also taught me that if you set goals, and work hard to achieve them—the hard work will pay off."

Another great example is of a thirteen-year-old boy who was six feet, eight inches tall, weighed 250 pounds, and wore a size 17 shoe. He was told he was too slow, too clumsy, and his feet were too big. He was also told that he would never be a basketball player and that he should be a goalie in soccer.

Today he is one of the greatest centers ever to play the game of basketball. His name is Shaquille O'Neal. Because he received some great encouragement from another coach (Dale Brown) and he listened to his own internal self, he continues to play in the NBA.

One last example is of an athlete who almost decided to give up on his dream of playing professional baseball. One Thanksgiving, he was with his wife's family and he was contemplating giving up on baseball. He was unable to see it going much further for him, or at least the way he thought it should be going for him. His family encouraged him to continue because he was getting paid to play the game he loved, even though it was a minimal salary.

The next spring, he was brought up to the big leagues, the MLB. For the next ten years, he had the best ten years of any player ever. He was voted by ESPN as the greatest player of the decade from 2000–2009. He is on pace to be one of the greatest ever and maybe *the* greatest ever. He is also on the verge of becoming the highest-paid baseball player ever. His name is Albert Pujols.

All three of these Warriors faced obstacles that made them contemplate giving up and quitting. They persevered to find, embrace, and be the best that they could be and are. They found their Warrior greatness.

Warrior excellence means calling forth the best from yourself. This is innately fulfilling. Living in integrity and doing your best is honoring your personal values and code of conduct. Those who strive diligently towards excellence, integrity, and high standards are generally happier, more financially success-ful, and more well-balanced, especially for the long term. Those who compromise excellence, integrity, and standards may appear to win in the short term, and they will ultimately face consequences and conflicts. I previously shared how I person-ally faced this for myself.

While the external world offers benchmarks of excellence, integrity, and standards, the real test is *inside* you. You know inside when you have really given something your all. You know when you have crossed an integrity line for yourself. You know when you have lowered a standard. It all comes down to you.

When you compromise your excellence, integrity, or standards, the result is a feeling inside that tells you something is off. Sometimes you attempt to fool yourself or are innocently seduced to com-promise a value, and you learn to justify your actions by saying "the end justifies the means" or "others are doing it." Perhaps you feel that your action is your only choice. Any action like this will begin a cycle of lowering standards. The cost is that it will move you further away from your true self, your ultimate purpose, long-lasting success, and your sense of fulfillment. This is one of the most essential ingredients to living the Warrior life you choose.

The first part of coming from your best is having personal integ-rity. It is to be true to yourself in all things. Be true to the very best that is in you. Being true to yourself means doing what you do in an excellent fashion. Integrity is demonstrated internally by personal honesty and externally by the quality of your actions.

Instead of winning, what if from now on your objective were to choose to do the very best of which you are capable? How much better would you perform? More importantly, how much better would you feel? What would your life be like if you refused to settle merely for winning—chasing material items, chasing accomplishments—and insisted instead on the peace of mind and the self-satisfaction that comes from knowing you have made the effort to do *your* best?

So much of what passes for success is a matter of how you appear to other people. You might be able to fool others with less than *your* best effort. You will always know whether you gave *your* best effort. This is the truth coaches Wooden, Brown, and Lombardi recommended we all live by.

Your decision to become excellent at what you do and to always give your best is a major key to great success. It is also the foundation of high levels of self-esteem and self-respect. When you are really good at what you do, you feel wonderful about yourself. It affects your entire personality and all of your relationships with other people when you know you are at the top of your game. It is the core of your Warrior greatness.

What is Warrior greatness? Warrior greatness is living and being your best. It is enjoying the challenge even when things become very difficult. Warriors are competitors. They understand and know it is exhilarating to be involved in something that is very challenging. They embrace it.

> ## Coming from your best creates your Warrior greatness. —MEL CERVENY
>
> ■ ■ ■

Warriors bravely step forward when others are afraid. They thrive when others wither. A Warrior chooses to be the point person in leading the way. After all, who is better suited to lead the cause? Warriors believe it is up to them, that this is *their* opportunity to shine—and they do.

Napoleon Hill said in the book *Think and Grow Rich,* "The majority of people are ready to throw their aims and purposes overboard and give up at the first sign of opposition or misfortune. A few carry on despite all opposition until they attain their goal."

Let's face it, struggles are necessary. They are God's way of allowing us to expand, develop, progress, and become stronger. Warriors persevere. Warriors have the ability to change their circumstances in life.

Warriors have always known persistence and perseverance are key ingredients in success. Recent psychological research has backed this up. Studies of entrepreneurs show that those who succeed possess a tremendous level of perseverance. They stick at it, even when the going gets tough and when others tell them to stop. Single-mindedness, determination, dedication, self-belief, and the ability to persevere distinguish people who do great things with their lives from those whose dreams die with them. When you have great perseverance, you remain true to your vision.

Warriors honor their own commitments. Commitment, persistence, and willpower are traits of Warriors. When these ingredients are cultivated and applied, success results. The reverse is also true. Lack of a firm commitment and little persistence to overcome real or fancied obstacles are two of the major causes of failure and disappointment.

The only things you are able to control are your thoughts, words, and actions. You determine how you respond to challenges, difficulties, and setbacks. The good news is that every time you respond in a positive and constructive manner, you become stronger and more knowledgeable. You are more capable of dealing with the next situation, challenge, difficulty, or setback that comes along. Whatever the obstacle put in your path, you will recognize or find a way to go over it, under it, around it, through it, or simply just let it be. Just do the best you are able to. If you fall short of the mark, do it again.

> ## "I always succeed by coming from my best." Say that to yourself one more time.
>
> ■ ■ ■

"Failing" is simply a judgment you or others place upon you. Doing your best, you may indeed fall short of someone else's expectations. Who cares? Doing your best and giving your best effort *is* the best you are able to do.

In the event you do something and realize afterwards that you could do better, then you are always able to choose again. In most cases, you may require practice, practice, and more practice before you are operating at your best.

Identify one skill that will help you the most, and then choose the appropriate action for yourself. Ask yourself this question: "What one skill, if I developed and did in an excellent fashion, would have the greatest positive impact on my life and on the lives of others?"

The external world places so much focus and attention on winning, losing, and failing. This may seem to be so paralyzing that most people avoid choosing to do their best or choosing any type of action; it's all fear-related. Winning or losing, and failing or succeeding are simply ways society compares and keeps score.

There is one easy way to drain your mental energy: compare yourself with or to others. Comparing yourself with others will provide you with one of two things: either you will feel proud when you are above or you will feel jealous, intimidated, fearful, or insecure when you are below. And, as we know, all are negative emotions and are all ego.

> ## Failing is simply a judgment you or others place upon you.
>
> ■ ■ ■

Our culture is full of comparisons. People like to compare themselves to others. While some people may say that comparing is a way to motivate yourself, it is still a form of placing judgment upon yourself. You know when you are performing at your best. Why worry about comparing yourself to others?

Are you doing your best? Or are you merely competing, comparing, and scoring yourself based on what others do? If so, why? All you have to do is perform at your best. You and only you control what you are doing. It is a choice. You have the power to do so. Start right now.

Remember, doing your best requires practice, practice, practice. Put on your socks, shoes, and lace them up and be your Warrior best. You are the best. I believe in you.

Are you choosing the effort to do the very best of which you are capable?

■ ■ ■

WARRIOR ACTION STEPS

■ ■ ■

YOUR WARRIOR GREATNESS.

Are you ready to accept fully the person you are?

1. Check in with yourself. Ask yourself the following questions:

    a. Where am I coming from my best? List three areas in which you are coming from your best.

    b. Am I applying my best effort to everything I do? List three things you are applying your best effort to.

    c. What do I choose to do differently? List three things you choose to do differently.

2. Be true to the very best that is in you. Practice. Practice. Practice. List three things you are able to practice more of.

3. Always live up to the very best that you are.

4. Say this to yourself daily: "I always succeed by coming from my best."

5. Stop comparing yourself to others. Name three things you do to compare yourself to others.

6. Find and align yourself with a mentor or coach, and be coachable. Set a date when you will find a mentor or coach.

■ ■ ■

Be Bold, Be Playful, Be Powerful, and Enjoy Your Great Warrior Adventure!

CHAPTER FIFTEEN

■ ■ ■

Surround Yourself with the Right People

You know when you are around the right people for you. You also know when you are around the wrong people for you. Be around the people who will honor you.

■ ■ ■

As I previously shared, Coach Dale Brown once asked me, "Outside of God grabbing ahold of you, to what do you attribute coming out of depression and away from being suicidal?" I responded, "Coach, simply getting around the *right* people."

I chose to be around people who saw in me what I failed to see for myself and who truly cared for me, wanted the best for me, and believed in me. I was fortunate to get around people who saw me for who I was. They saw me for where I was, and they saw it as a new starting point for me.

Being around the right people has a major impact on who we are, what we do, and how we live within the external world. You know when you are around the right people for you.

You also know when you are around the wrong people. These people simply share different views and values. They have different beliefs or understanding in some or all of your own choices. At virtually every turning point in your life, someone is standing there to either help you or hinder you. Some of the wrong people for you are sometimes those closest to you. They may care about you, and they are at a place in which they are unable to provide authentic and loving support.

Our lives are shaped and influenced by a myriad of factors. Relationships are at the top of the list. Think about how much of "who you are today" has been influenced by a specific parent, sibling, relative, teacher, coach, neighbor, associate, celebrity, athlete, author, speaker, boss, coworker, spouse, or friend. Values, habits, behavior, knowledge, skills, passions, hobbies, tastes, and attitudes are typically learned through association with others.

A variety of individuals make up your "circle of influence." Some are negative, and others are simply neutral bystanders. Often you are blessed with enriching associations that positively affect your life. Just being present to the impact someone has on your state of being is powerful. Are you aware of the impact people in your life are having on you?

People who come into your life may be in your life for a moment, a season, or a lifetime. The majority of the success and happiness you will have in life is determined by the quality of the relationships that you develop and surround yourself with, both in your personal and business activities. The more people know you in a positive way and are truly supportive of you, the more success you will have. You will be able to move much more swiftly in your life.

Warriors choose a habit of building and maintaining a network of high-quality relationships throughout their lives. They surround themselves with people who are supportive of them and who believe in them. Virtually all of your great successes in life will be accompanied by great relationships with people who help you and whom you help in return.

When you choose to elevate your success, associate yourself with positive people. Associate with people who are positive, optimistic, happy, grounded, and who have goals and are moving forward in their lives—people who will provide uplifting and authentic support of you and who believe in you. People who will tell you the truth.

At the same time, get away from negative, critical, complaining people. Are you able to fly with eagles when scratching with the turkeys? Be around positive people. 1 Corinthians 15:33 says: "Do not be deceived: Bad company corrupts good morals." Having good company creates positive flow and good morals.

Stay away from those people who are attempting to act as if they are your friends when what they are really doing is bringing you down. They are pulling you in the wrong direction, away from honoring your true self. They do this by encouraging you to do things you know are things that you disapprove of. It is quite easy to become chameleon-like and choose to have the attitudes, behaviors, values, and beliefs of the people with whom you associate most often.

> **The more grounded, centered, and secure in who you are, the easier it is to allow life to flow for you.**
>
> ■ ■ ■

It is well-known that a group of electric batteries will provide more energy than a single battery. It is also well-known that an individual battery will provide energy in proportion to the number and capacity of the cells it contains.

Human brains function similarly to an electric battery. It absorbs energy and translates that energy into matter. This accounts for the fact that some brains are more efficient than others, leading to this significant statement: "A group of brains coordinated or connected in a spirit of harmony will provide more thought energy than a single brain, just as a group of electric batteries will provide more energy than a single battery."

When Coach Brown became the head coach at LSU, he surrounded himself with men of commitment and character: coaches Jack Schalow, who went on to become the associate head coach of the Portland Trailblazers, and Homer Drew, the legendary head coach at Valparaiso. Coach Brown also sought out the council and mentorship of two of the greatest coaches of all time, John Wooden and Adolph Rupp. Coach Brown became a successful coach by allying himself with great minds whose vibrations of thought he absorbed into his own mind, creating positive action and helping him become a Hall of Fame coach.

Coach Brown added to his own brain power with the sum and substance of the intelligence, experience, knowledge, and spiritual forces of these men. Moreover, he appropriated and made use of surrounding himself with like-minded Warriors.

Warriors use the power of thought and actions of those with whom they associate in a spirit of energy, empathy, and harmony. Warriors align themselves with others of like mind. Jesus had His twelve disciples. Napoleon Hill referred to this as the "Master Mind Alliance." He defined this as "a coordination of knowledge and effort, in a spirit of harmony, between two or more people, for the attainment of a definite purpose." This principle is available to you.

A properly chosen Warrior alliance creates an intangible potential of power. There are two characteristics of the alliance, one of which is economic in nature and the other of which is psychic.

The economic feature is obvious. Economic advantages may be created by any person who surrounds himself with the advice, counsel, and personal cooperation of a group of Warriors who are willing to lend wholehearted aid in a spirit of *perfect harmony*. This form of cooperative alliance has been the basis of nearly every great success or fortune. Your understanding of this great truth will definitely determine your Warrior success.

Choose to inventory the five closest friends with whom you associate yourself. It is almost a certainty you are somewhere in the middle of them in terms of your values, beliefs, and present economic situation. When you choose to have higher values, beliefs, and more money, be around more successful Warriors.

The psychic phase of your Warrior alliance is more abstract and requires much more understanding to comprehend. This is because it has reference to the spiritual forces.

Keep in mind that there are only two known elements in the entire universe—energy and matter. It is well-known that matter may be broken down into units of molecules, atoms, and electrons. Units of matter may be isolated, separated, and analyzed. Likewise, there are units of energy. The human mind is a form of energy, with part of it being spiritual in nature. When the minds of two people are coordinated in a *spirit of harmony*, the spiritual units of energy of each mind form an affinity, which constitutes the "psychic" phase of the Warrior alliance.

With every plan you adopt in your life, you must "listen to your inner self." Once you have done this, the joint creation of yourself and every member of your Warrior alliance may assist you in providing additional insight for your direction and plans.

The trusted allies you choose to surround yourself with must be chosen for their ability to help you to where you are going. They must truly care about you and believe in you. They must provide honest, encouraging, and nonjudgmental support.

Good company creates good morals.

■ ■ ■

I have learned by experience that merely liking a person is a poor reason to have him or her as a member of your inner Warrior alliance. It is okay to have such a person in your life, if his or her contribution may simply be this very friendship you appreciate.

Good communication and clarity creates definiteness, power, and positive actions by you. To receive the full benefit of your Warrior alliance, keep in constant and continuous contact with them. Communication should be scheduled often. The focus of the alliance should be definiteness of purpose, with a positive plan backed by continuous peace and harmony. The major strength of such an alliance consists in the balanced blending of the minds of all Warriors.

Jealousy, envy, judgment, or friction, as well as lagging of interest, on the part of any member will bring defeat. If this happens, remove that person from your alliance. Set and honor the boundaries that work for you.

By carrying out these instructions with persistence, intelligence, and discrimination in the selection of your Warrior alliance, your objective will be reached, even before you begin to recognize it.

The very best way to network and build your relationships is to look constantly for ways to help other people achieve their own goals, dreams, and aspirations. The more you give of yourself without expecting something in return, the more rewards will come back to you in the most unexpected sources.

People enjoy helping people they like. When you have a sincere like for people, people will like you. Ditch the "what's-in-it-for-me" attitude. Cultivate a genuine care and concern for others.

By assisting others, they will assist you. When you give of yourself, when you provide genuine help to people, you will receive far more in return.

Choose to be around the right people for you. Start selecting your Warrior alliance today.

Are you around the right people for you?

■ ■ ■

WARRIOR ACTION STEPS

■ ■ ■

SURROUND YOURSELF WITH THE RIGHT PEOPLE

The Warrior alliance has assisted every individual who has experienced any type of success or greatness.

1. Choose to inventory people who are in your life. Create a list of who has a positive influence and who has a negative influence on you. Are these people supportive of you and your purpose?

2. Set the necessary boundaries for what is best for you with the people in your life. Honor yourself.

3. Understand the power of positive associations and rub some elbows.

   a. Be around people who believe in you.

   b. Be around people who are positive.

   c. Be around people who are supportive of you.

   d. Keep negative people out of your life or at least at arm's length.

4. Find and align yourself with positive people. Form your very own Warrior alliance with like-minded Warriors.

5. Schedule routine time with them.

■ ■ ■

Be Bold, Be Playful, Be Powerful, and Enjoy Your Great Warrior Adventure!

CHAPTER SIXTEEN

■   ■   ■

Have Big, Big Goals, Dreams, and Aspirations

When the mind of a Warrior is ready to conceive and believe, he is able to achieve.

■   ■   ■

The starting point for all achievement is desire. Focus on whatever you choose to have in life—your goals, dreams, and aspirations. Strong desires are the catalyst to produce more intense and sustained action on your part. Armed with a strong desire, you will be able to overcome the inevitable obstacles and detours between where you are and where you choose to be.

Having big, big goals, dreams, and aspirations provides you with a powerful imagination. Dreams and aspirations tap into a source of magnificent possibility and energy. They provide you the power to accomplish what you have imagined. When you think in terms of goals, dreams, and aspirations together, you give yourself the inspirational edge you require to have your thoughts come true.

What's YOUR dream?

■ ■ ■

Goals, dreams, and aspirations are visions of success and happiness in the future. They are representations of the "good life" to come. Our ability to think first of dreams and setting goals forms a base for the process of our later achievements. It provides us something to strive for. Everything achieved is first conceived as an idea. You have the ability to start, or restart, whatever it is you choose, right now.

Daydreaming is a natural part of living, a hope for a better future, something to anticipate. Our dreams evolve and crystallize as our desire becomes stronger. Desire is the motivation and the necessary launching pad for the accomplishment of any goal. Through the repetitive thought process of desire, hazy dreams and aspirations will become specific goals. Goals are essential because goals make us go. Goals are the fuel in your tank.

After all, what is a goal? It is a dream with a target date. What is a dream? A vision that fills our mind. An aspiration? A strong desire or longing.

What do you get when you put these together? You receive energy to go and accomplish them.

Having desire for your goals, dreams, and aspirations and going after them with intense action and definiteness of purpose creates a powerful force and a powerful energy within you.

Desire and *definiteness* create *energy*. The energy created by desire and definiteness spills over to all areas of your life. It creates the necessary burning desire within you.

Maintain a burning desire. I have been a consistent goal setter since I was a child. Any time I set a goal and was laser-focused upon it, I would achieve it. Sometimes I missed the desired goal date. When I stayed focused and knew what the action steps were to achieve a goal, I eventually hit it. How? I was simply laser-focused upon the desired goal, and I knew exactly what I had to do to achieve it.

I laid out what was required to achieve my goal, how to have it or achieve it, and in what time frame I desired to accomplish it. I would share my goals with other people. I thought about them. I talked about them. I never let anything get in the way accomplishing what I desired to have. This created an energy that led to accomplishment and attainment. The only times I missed hitting my desired goals were due to one of two reasons: I decided to change my mind about going after the goal, or I simply was unsure of what to do or how to go about achieving a certain step or process.

I have witnessed countless people who are afraid to start going after their goals, dreams, and aspirations. They are fearful of failure, fearful of what others will say. They seem to require some type of permission. Go ahead and give yourself permission to go after what you choose to have. Go ahead. Do it. Choose the actions necessary for yourself.

> **A burning desire to be and to do is the starting point from which the dreamer must start.**
>
> ■ ■ ■

With everything you have learned about yourself in this book, you have the ability to go after everything you desire. You also have God the Almighty on your side and a community of like-minded Warriors around to assist you. All you have to do is determine what it is you desire and start choosing action. Awake, arise, and assert yourself.

Dreams are chosen from a simple thought and turned into an action of what the dreamer desires. Be the dreamer of the world. Be the dreamer of the world with action. Go for what you desire. Give yourself permission to soar. Give yourself permission to choose action and to go for it.

If you fall, it is okay. Just like the Frank Sinatra song says, "Pick yourself up, dust yourself off, and start all over again." The world has become accustomed to new discoveries. Go create your new discoveries.

> **Anyone who does anything worthwhile anywhere has followed through on his or her goals.**
>
> ■ ■ ■

In 1953, Yale University surveyed its graduating class and discovered that only 3 percent had written goals. Twenty years later, Yale surveyed this same class and learned that the 3 percent who had written goals, had amassed a net worth greater than that of the other 97 percent combined.

I find it amazing to know that 97 percent of the people of the world are drifting aimlessly through life, without goals and the slightest concept of how powerful they are if they would look within, find what they are best suited for, and create a goal-oriented lifestyle.

Warriors have developed goal-centered lifestyles in which their goals are part of their day-to-day lives. The benefit to choosing this way of life is that it creates a more focused and fulfilling life.

When Warriors choose to do something, *they do so*. A small percentage of the population choose to live their lives this way. The rest choose the alternative, which leads to missed opportunities and life just passing them by.

There is a psychological as well as an economic reason for the selection of a definite purpose or aim in life. Any definite purpose or aim that is deliberately fixed in the mind and held there, with the determination to realize it, finally saturates the entire subconscious mind until it automatically influences the physical action of the body toward the attainment of that purpose.

When you have a goal, dream, or aspiration and a definite purpose or aim in life, be clear about what it will require to accomplish it. Once selected, have it written out and placed where you will see it daily. The psychological effect of this is to impress this purpose upon your subconscious mind so strongly that it accepts the purpose as a pattern or blueprint that will eventually dominate your activities in life and lead you, step by step, toward the attainment.

Every great Warrior, from the dawn of civilization to the present, was a dreamer. All Warriors have the vision and the imagination to see realities in their mental and spiritual form before they are transmuted into physical form. All great Warriors begin with a dream of something wonderful and different from where they were when they first had the dream or aspiration.

Imagine being able to achieve, be, have, or do whatever you choose in life. Just for the moment, imagine you have all the time, resources, money, education, experience, friends, contacts, and everything else you need to achieve anything you desire in life. When your potential is completely unlimited, what kind of a life would you choose to create for yourself?

You may as well know, right here, that for you to have what you desire, you must create a white heat of desire for it and actually *believe* you will possess it. What this means is that when you have a desire, the energy is sent out into the universe, and your consciousness makes this work. The energy is God, and God is our collective consciousness. God, our creator, loves us in such a way as to give us abundance and to feel immense joy at our receiving these gifts and joy when we give abundantly to each other. It is through immense faith and belief, fueled with the power of our minds and emotions, that the law works in our lives.

As previously discussed, the use of conscious language is a key way for you to start transcending your goals, dreams, and aspirations into reality. This is so they are moving toward you. You may ask, "What do you mean about moving toward you?" It means you are attracting everything to you in every moment, mostly by default. You are able to attract everything by your design. Being present with your thoughts and words will create the focus, attention, and energy for what you desire, and it *will* come to you. What is especially important is to just let everything be and be open to receiving.

> ## I have the power to do and achieve what I desire.
>
> ■ ■ ■

Imagine trusting in God, yourself, and in your infinite possibilities. Imagine receiving everything you choose to have in your life. God created us out of an immense joy in the act of creation and gave us "free will" to then, with joy, watch us create for ourselves the lives we have chosen, both consciously and unconsciously.

Ecclesiastes 5:19 reads, "Furthermore, as for every man to whom God has given riches and wealth, He has also empowered him to eat from them and to receive his reward and rejoice in his labor; this is the gift of God."

Sounds easy, right? Ask for what you would like. What do you desire to attract right now? Children ask for things all the time. They tell themselves they can have it. They focus on it and stay focused on what they choose to have. They leave the how to the adults. They ask and they ask and they drive the adults crazy until they receive what they desire.

So, what specifically do you choose to have in your life? What is one thing you desire right now? Imagine that you have this thing you have chosen or this way of being you have chosen. How do you feel? Deeply embrace the feeling of this outcome. When you do this, you will be feeling pretty excited. The more feeling and passion you put into your desires, the stronger your internal desire will be. The more focused you are, the higher you raise your energy and remind yourself of where you are going, the faster what you are asking for will happen for you.

This is where your environment and being in the present moment are such powerful keys. Warriors always tend to move in the direction of their dominant dreams, images, and visions. The very act of allowing yourself to have big, big goals, dreams, and aspirations actually raises your awareness.

It improves your self-concept and increases your level of self-confidence. It increases your personal level of self-respect and personal happiness. There is something about dreams and visions that is exciting and stimulates you to come from your best.

Knowing you could absolutely be guaranteed of success in any one thing in life, large or small, short-term or long-term, what would it be? What one great thing would you dare to dream if you knew you would achieve it? Warriors think about their goals, dreams, and aspirations most of the time. As a result, they are continually moving toward them. Whatever you think about most of the time grows and increases in your life, both positively and negatively. Focus on *what you choose to have* versus what you do not choose to have or what you lack. Be positive in your thoughts, words, and actions (conscious language).

When you are visualizing, thinking, and talking about your goals, dreams, and aspirations, you tend to accomplish far more in life. Warriors know how and where they are going.

Know where you're going. Do you know where you are going? Without knowing where you are going, you may end up somewhere else. When you have big, big goals, dreams, and aspirations, it is important to determine your plan of action for achieving them. Create your road map. The more specific you are, the more likely you are to organize yourself around achieving them. Your attainment is much easier knowing what to do, how to do it, and when you are going to do it by. Being specific creates a much easier understanding of the process for attainment.

> **Create a burning desire for what you choose to have or achieve, and it will be yours.**
>
> ■ ■ ■

The Achievement Process

As previously stated, the starting point for all achievement is desire. Strong desires are the catalyst to produce more intense and sustained action on your part. The steps (provided by Napoleon Hill in *Think and Grow Rich*) to developing commitment and persistence, are as follows:

1. Desire. A definite purpose backed by a burning desire for its fulfillment;

2. Goals. The ability to first think of dreams, and set goals, forms a base for the process of our later achievements;

3. Planning. A definite plan, expressed in continuous action;

4. Belief. The ability to have absolute faith and conviction that your desires, goals, and plans will be conceived. A mind closed tightly against all negative suggestions of others, and;

5. Action. Choosing to act consciously with physical and mental activity.

The first two stages, *desire* (dreams) and *goals,* are necessary prerequisites to stage three, *planning.* To merely dream and have no plan is wishful thinking. Determining a course of action and establishing a timetable for achievement are essential ingredients in planning.

The fourth stage, *belief,* is conviction, faith, and confidence in the truth or existence of something. Belief is the ability to have absolute faith and conviction that your *desire, goals,* and *planning* will be conceived. The future belongs to those who believe in their dreams. Belief is the one basic and absolutely essential ingredient in successful Warriors.

As Dr. David Schwartz says in *The Magic of Thinking Big*:

> Every human being desires success. Some of the most practical success-building wisdom is found in the biblical scriptures stating that faith can move mountains . . . You can move a mountain with belief. You simply will have success by believing you will succeed. Strong belief triggers the mind to figuring ways and means and the "how to." Believing you will succeed allows others to place confidence in you.

One of the most powerful forces in the world is the will of the Warrior who believes in himself, who aims high, and who confidently goes after the things he chooses from life . . . "I am, I am able, and I will." The gap between what a man thinks he will achieve and what is actually possible to him is very, very small. First he must believe that he will.

All hopes, dreams, goals, plans, beliefs, and yes, even prayers, may be lost without the fifth stage of the achievement process—*action.* Ask yourself this question: "Am I serious about my true desires to choose action? Sustained action turns *desire* into a reality.

As a powerful Warrior creator, go create and live your big, big goals, dreams, and aspirations. How big, big are your goals, dreams, and aspirations? Are you ready to go after them?

Choose action now.

■ ■ ■

WARRIOR ACTION STEPS

■ ■ ■

HAVE BIG, BIG GOALS, DREAMS, AND ASPIRATIONS

Give yourself permission to go for your goals, dreams, and aspirations.

1. Dream Big. Big. HUGE. Give yourself permission to go for your goals, dreams, and aspirations.

2. What do you desire? Know what you desire. Determine what specific goals you choose to achieve. Then dedicate yourself to their attainment with purpose and the strong zeal of a Warrior. Develop a sincere burning desire for the things you choose to have in life. A burning desire is the greatest motivator of every human action. The desire for success implants "success consciousness" which, in turn, creates a vigorous and ever-increasing "habit of success." Write your goals down and share them with someone.

3. Develop a plan for achieving your goal and a deadline or target date for its attainment. Plan your progress carefully, day by day and month by month. Organized activity and maintained enthusiasm are the wellsprings of your power. Perform the necessary short-term steps, and know when to adjust your plan.

4. Stay focused on the short-term steps and the long-term outcomes. Visualize victory right now, and imagine the benefit or achievement of them.

5. Choose constant and continuous action toward them.

■ ■ ■

Be Bold, Be Playful, Be Powerful, and Enjoy Your Great Warrior Adventure!

CHAPTER SEVENTEEN

■ ■ ■

Live in the Now

All you are able to do is live right now. No matter what you think about the past or plan for the future, you still have to live this very moment. Live and enjoy right now.

■ ■ ■

O f all of the steps in this book, this is the one I have had to work on the most. I have always been great at being so focused on accomplishing tasks and responsibilities right now that I often will choose to delay embracing, enjoying, or living in the present moment. In the past, I was simply doing in the present moment. My mindset was, "I will get this completed now so I am able to enjoy it tomorrow or at some designated time in the future." I would have fun and enjoy my life later.

Nothing exists outside this present moment. That is a very different way of thinking than I was used to. I have learned and finally embraced focusing on and living in the now. *Living happens in the present moment. Fulfillment happens in the present moment.*

Most people spend their time complaining about the past or worrying about the future. Do you know anyone like this? We live in a fast-paced world, and the concept of slowing down and appreciating each moment may seem like a waste of time. However, it is in the present moment where you will find fulfillment and joy. It is simply about "being present" to everything and anything in the here and the now. It is about being present to the experience and accepting it and living now, *right now*.

Having acceptance simply means *embracing what is*. Acknowledging the "what" may include yourself, your spouse, significant other, job, house, life, health, and prosperity, or a set of circumstances. With acceptance, embrace peace. It is in this peace where your magnificence will happen.

When you accept something, you let go of the resistance, the fight, or the struggle. What is left is peace. It is this resistance to "what is" that keeps you in a locked set of behaviors. When you resist circumstances in your life, your energy is tied up in the struggle. As soon as you just accept the circumstances, the energy is free to move about. You are able to dance with "what is" in a different way, often creating the very movement you are looking for.

Many years ago, one of my goals was to become very wealthy. I figured that would be a positive goal to achieve, one that would give me a lot more freedom and happiness. When I gazed into the future, I saw the potential for wealth and freedom. I thought that to reach that goal, I would have to endure a definite absence of enjoying the present.

Then one day, one of my friends and coaches Greg Klein said, "You are doing a magnificent job in doing and accomplishing tasks." Right then my ego felt great. I was thinking to myself, "Thanks for noticing." Then he handed me a bat so I could swing it, and I did. The bat was swung to my head and hit me like a ton of bricks. He said, "Do you mind if I share an observation with you? You are doing such a great job of doing, you seem to be living and enjoying the future." Right then was a major "aha" moment for me. He was right, and I knew exactly what he meant. I was so caught up in doing, I was choosing to live my life later.

The irony of this is that I have always enjoyed just having fun. When I was focused upon a task or responsibility or a goal I had set, I would become so focused on the "future" accomplishment that I would become very direct, rigid, and, in many cases, uptight or stressed. All because I was doing. Constant go, go, go and do, do, do. I was on autopilot of just doing. Then I learned from a statement from one of my dear friends, Janet Kelly, that constant do, do, do creates "doo-doo." Over time it starts to smell. Wow. Are you able to relate with all of your doing? Are you creating "doo-doo" for yourself?

> ## Living happens in the
> ## present moment.
>
> ■ ■ ■

My closest friends, family, and associates admired and loved how I was great at accomplishing what I set out to do. The challenge for my friends, family, and associates was that they disliked the intensity I would have in these moments. By all of my doing, I actually was hurting many of my closest relationships. Initially this plan of delayed gratification seemed sensible and intelligent to me. I thought I had to choose sacrifices of delayed gratification while I was young to create a better future for myself.

My intellect liked the way I operated, and my intuition kept fighting it. I experienced a major head-versus-soul battle as I pondered the issue of sacrificing freedom in the present to achieve greater freedom in the future. I figured it was just a matter of discipline and self-sacrifice and that, in the long run, all my efforts would pay off.

In many cases during my life, all of this delayed gratification and hard work did, in fact, have a payoff for me. Unfortunately, inside I was paying a price. The more success I had, the more unfulfilled I was. I loved the sense of accomplishment and the fulfillment. I had chosen to overlook the fact that all of this accomplishment was a temporary fulfillment. It was like a drug, and each time, I had to go for more and do it faster. There was a significant amount of joy simply in the chase.

I was addicted to more accomplishment. Then I realized I was an addict. Yes, an addict. You may ask how that could be. Well, the truth is, I was.

Let's discuss what addiction is. *Addiction is the giving away of yourself.* Anytime you give a piece of yourself away, it is a form of addiction. I was giving away many parts of myself, and I was also clearly giving away my present moment for the future, which was clearly an illusion.

My addiction also created another issue for me—fear. I was so afraid of failing or falling back or miss accomplishing what I set out to do that it created even more intensity and detachment from myself. The fear of failing to achieve or win was greater than my sense of accomplishment.

All of my accomplishment was in the future. After each accomplishment, I would ask myself, "What am I able to start doing now to get what I desire in the future?" It was a constant cycle. Rinse, wash, rinse, dry, and repeat, over and over.

During this process, I created so much stress for myself. The chase and the constant doing became mundane for me. I became numb to the process. I began to push my feelings deeper down inside me. I became detached from myself.

I was caught up in the illusion of control as well. I had to be in control of the process to get to the accomplishment and meet the expectations I had set for myself. I thought for a long while about how I was either in control or I was out of control, and I realized my entire life was simply out of control.

I was out of control in everything in my life. All of the perceived control was all an illusion. It created undue stress and conflict within me and, in many circumstances, my internal conflict was projected externally as well.

Over time, I started to realize internally that this was a behavior of creating my very own insanity. I asked myself, "How am I able to enjoy this process now? How am I able to be and live in the now?"

I rarely was in the present moment. I was living in the future. I discovered a major illusion when I finally understood that all I have is this very moment. I was unable to live in the past or the future. After years of hard work and encountering some major roadblocks along the way, I was falling shorter and shorter of where I desired to be, even though the external world was saying I was exactly where I was supposed to be.

Maybe you are in the same position right now. Do you know the saying, "Simply be"? I truly never understood this. What do you mean, "Just be"? I would think, "I do not want to be. I want to do. I want to go. I want to accomplish. I want to go after my goals, dreams, and aspirations. I desire to just go, go, go and do, do, do."

I found out that by being in and enjoying the here and now, I am creating my reality now and in the future. All of my go, go, go and do, do, do was only creating more chaos and conflict in my life. The ego said go, and my center and true, authentic self said, "Enjoy the moment right now. Be present now."

> **Constant go, go, go and do, do, do creates "doo-doo."** —Janet Kelly
>
> ■　■　■

My ego and my center were at conflict, and I was too busy going and doing to see what was really going on. Are you too busy to see and hear what your true center is telling you? This very moment is guaranteed. We have to live right now in this very moment. Are you living and enjoying this very moment?

By living my life in the moment, I began to experience a freedom I had never thought possible. I started to let go of worry, fear, and things I had no control over. After all, worry and fear are products of attachment to the past or the future. Once the attachment is released, worry and fear are also released.

As human beings, we tend to waste our consciousness by living outside the present moment. In the run of the day, our thoughts are often fixed upon either the past or the future. The mind registers only a minimal amount of what is taking place in the here and now. As a result of this tendency to function on autopilot, much of the wonder and beauty of life passes us by unnoticed. For instance, when you travel on a plane, bus, or train, you are more likely to spend the trip thinking about your destination than appreciating the passing scenery, even though you are gazing out the window.

How often do you find yourself replaying the events of the day at the dinner table, mulling over what-ifs and should-haves' as you chew and swallow your food absentmindedly, as if you were in a hypnotic state? Are you so intent on looking either forward or backward at life that you go through much of it as if in a dream, with a limited awareness of present reality?

Imagine the last conversation you had with someone. Were you thinking about what you had to do or forgot to do? Were you in the present moment listening intently to the other person? Was your mind somewhere else?

Now imagine this same conversation. This time you know the other person is somewhere else in his or her thoughts. The other person is preoccupied, only acting as if he or she is there. The person is also in the past or somewhere in the future. He or she is somewhere else other than being in the moment with you. How do you feel knowing this?

Are you being present in your conversations with yourself and with others? Are you hearing and listening? Are you present?

When you were a child, you experienced life in the now. Providing your needs were all met, you had little reason to concern yourself with the past or worry about your future. You experienced the fresh edge of wonder at each new discovery of your world. You existed and lived in the present moment. You lived and enjoyed the simplicity of life. Do you remember this?

As you grew into an adult, that feeling of awe diminished because you become caught up in the effort of survival and the demands of your life and time. You spent at least eight hours of every day at some form of employment. When you were outside of work, you were concerned with other necessities and responsibilities of your life—after-hour appointments, social commitments, the demands of children and spouses. You increasingly engaged your own autopilot, which allowed you to function physically while jumping ahead mentally to the next task or responsibility. After a while, this became a habitual mode of existence, and your awareness of the world around you narrowed because you were rarely fully present in the moment. In effect, you began to function like a robot or a sleepwalker in your waking life.

Are you able to relate? Are you living on autopilot? How do you break free from this habitual mode of functioning? How do you regain the sense of newness that will expand your mind and awaken you from your dream? You do it with intent. That is, you must exercise the full power of your human will and become mindful of every action you undertake. You must constantly be aware and remind yourself to pay close attention to your thoughts, words, and actions. Be present and embrace the sensation of chewing and tasting your food. Be present and feel your hands on the steering wheel and revel in the synchronistic movements of shifting gears. To enjoy the sounds, smells, and sights in your life, you must be present.

Even the simplest gestures such as smiling, shaking hands, or looking at your watch must be undertaken with the mind fully focused on the task. It is a conscious feat when you awaken to your own existence in the present now.

> **When you are "present,"**
> **you have power, and in that**
> **power, you have choice.**
>
> ■ ■ ■

Once you have allowed the consciousness to fall into a state of nonuse, it requires effort to regain its focus. Your consciousness will become stronger the more it is used. When you start to persevere, the rewards will be well worth the effort as your consciousness expands. You begin to embrace, live, and enjoy the here and now. The present moment. Your present moment. Life becomes an entirely different perspective for you. Are you ready?

When you begin to practice paying attention to and being mindful of what you are doing, you begin to have full use of your five senses. You are actually tasting your food, enjoying the sensations of movement, and discovering with wonder the many things around you that have previously gone unnoticed.

Your amazement at this phenomenon causes you to become aware of your previous sleeping state. The more you become aware of this, the more effort you will choose to put into remaining awake to your own experiences.

Life becomes fascinating once again as you regain your childlike sense of awe in everything you experience. When you begin to awaken, you begin to feel the happy exhilaration of being fully conscious in the present moment, and you begin to be fully alive in the now. When living your life in the present moment, you are experiencing a freedom. Worry and fear subside for you. After all, worry and fear are products of attachment to the past or the future (all a derivative of your ego). Once the attachment to the past or future is released, worry and fear are also released.

As you become more conscious of "staying in the moment," you will find yourself beginning to let go of your attachment to the future outcome of events in your life. Keep planning and setting your goals. Simply stop being attached to their outcome. Enjoy the process because it is amazing how much power flows in the attainment of them.

How do I proceed to live in the now? I recently had a conversation with one of my good friends and business partners, Blake Mallen (another high achiever). We were discussing how important it is to focus on your desired destination in life. Blake's personal license plate even reads "ENDNMND," representing the Steven Covey philosophy of "beginning with the end in mind." Blake also pointed out how he came to the same realization that I did about living in the now, or as he put it, "It is critical to know where you choose to go, and it is equally important to enjoy the process along the way. In the end, you realize that the *enjoyment of the process* is actually the main point!"

Learning to understand the *power of being and living in the now* and truly enjoying the present moment is a new way of living for most. This has definitely been the case for me. The past and the future are illusions. They only exist to the degree you focus your attention on them right now. You create the past and the future by imagining them in the present. You only exist in the very here and now.

For you, this might seem a logical difference. It was a radical new way of awareness and living for me. As I grasped the idea that nothing exists outside this present moment, I changed my overall life strategy. I understood that if I am to experience anything in life, I must create it in this moment. It must exist in some form right now. The idea of creating freedom, happiness, peace, and love in the future by constraining myself in the present was nothing more than a fool's choice. The future would never arrive as I saw fit for myself as long as I was creating confinement and scarcity in the here and now.

The future is certainly a convenient mental construct. I found that projecting too much of what I desired into my future was hurting the enjoyment of my present. What is the point of working to create a future of joy and freedom if my present reality is just the opposite? By choosing to have freedom, happiness, peace, and love in the future, I had to create it right here, right now. The only power I have to create anything is here in the present, right now.

This paradigm shift in thinking produced a significant shift in my priorities. I began to focus more of my energy on improving the quality of my present reality instead of projecting all those improvements into the realm of "someday." I started asking questions such as, "How am I able to I experience more joy in this very moment? What am I able to do right now and enjoy right now?"

> # Fulfillment happens in the present moment.
>
> ■ ■ ■

My present reality took some time for me to transform. It has greatly changed over the past several years. Because of my own past conditioning, I still find it is a process and a journey to constantly remember. I have to really focus and be aware of the here and now. As part of this process, I have stopped doing and going after everything in the future. I now live and accept living, being, and letting almost everything come to me. I am still committed to the process.

I have created my own reality by setting in motion this very moment my thoughts, words, and actions to bring my future goals, dreams, and aspirations to me. I also began to simply be, to live, and to teach right now. I have enjoyed my personal growth and development. I choose to pay it forward to others this very moment, right here, right now.

I still have goals, dreams, and aspirations. I have a plan, and I keep a calendar. I work very much the same way as before. I simply plan knowing everything is subject to change at a moment's notice. I accept changes, and I know in most cases any changes are small ripples in the water. I am still focused upon the destination and the end in mind. I understand what I am playing for, and I choose to be and enjoy the process.

I started to reduce my overhead costs. I got rid of unnecessary expenses. I quit buying frivolous items or buying multiple items. I simplified every part of my life. I have also minimized doing stressful deadline-oriented project work.

Now I am so passionate about my life and career. I am living *now* because I choose to share my life experiences with as many people as possible. I am going with the current of my life and with the flow. I look to my business to express my happiness outward and to share it with others.

I began to write and to create things that would have a positive impact upon me and on others. I started choosing more time off for myself. I began doing more things I enjoyed.

I have become less attached, stingy, and concerned with my possessions and money (however, I still teach and recommend responsibility of money.). I began to be less attached to outcomes or things I had no control over. I have more time to simply be and live. My life is more and more enjoyable.

I started choosing time to enjoy what was most important for me. Previously, I had placed my time behind others' time and responsibilities. I made a decision to choose my time for me. Time is one of our most precious assets. Are you using your asset of time for what is best for you?

> **One of the greatest gifts you are able to give to yourself and to others is being present.**
>
> ■   ■   ■

My friend Wayne McKamie recently shared a story with me. He said he had made arrangements to have his handyman do some work on a lamppost. The repairs required part of the lamppost to be replaced. Wayne and the handyman agreed to schedule a time for the handyman to come and replace the part.

Then on the scheduled day, it began to rain. So the handyman decided to pass on showing up to perform the work. Wayne said to himself, "How many times have I chosen to do something instead of choosing the time necessary? How many times did I allow an excuse to delay something? How many times did I value the importance of doing something other than what was scheduled?"

Wayne decided to go out into the rain and replace the part on the lamppost by himself. He figured he would choose the time, and he would accomplish the task.

A few days later, the handyman called Wayne and said he was ready to come over to replace the part on the lamppost. Wayne replied, "The part has been replaced." The handyman seemed confused and asked, "Who changed it and when?" Wayne answered, "I replaced it, and I replaced it on Saturday in the rain."

The handyman asked, "Why?" Wayne replied, "I decided my time is valuable. How many times had I chosen the time to do something else than for myself or for someone else? If I am going to find the time and, more importantly, choose to make the time, I must follow through with my plan. So, how was a little bit of rain a reason to prevent me from choosing the time to complete the task?"

The handyman failed to understand this reasoning. However, Wayne did. The point to this story is that we have all made excuses or decided to do things other than choosing the time to do something, whether for ourselves or someone else.

Wayne also shared with me another story about putting air in his car's tire. He asked me, "How many times have you had a low amount of air in your car's tire, knew it, and still waited to make the time to put some air in it?"

I said, "Wayne, I just put air in my car's tire within the past thirty minutes. I drove around for two days knowing I had a low tire. I simply chose the time, all two or three minutes to put some air in my car's tire."

We both agreed most people are simply surviving in this world, and they choose to wait to do what is necessary now. They know they should do it now, and they choose otherwise for themselves, even when they know it is best for them.

> **Worry and fear are products of attachment to the past or to the future.**
>
> ■ ■ ■

Time is one of your biggest assets. Are you choosing the necessary time or, more importantly, choosing the time for what is truly important for you? Choose your time wisely. Start living in the present moment. Simply start being. It becomes much more enjoyable to do so. Please choose the necessary adjustments for you.

I was initially concerned that focusing too much on the present moment, I would be shortsighted. My experience has been just the opposite. I started to choose the time required for *me* first. The more I focused on me, the more I began to accomplish, and the more I enjoyed it. I had a new sense of enjoyment.

I am still able to create plans for the future and work on long-term goals, dreams, and aspirations. In the past, I would set goals because I believed achieving those goals would increase my happiness. Now the flow goes in reverse. I go with the current of my life and what works for me. This lifestyle design has led me to be far more produc- tive and happier.

I have happiness, and because of this happiness, I achieve the goals, dreams, and aspirations I choose to have. Today, I set goals to increase the expression of my happiness and to assist others in transforming their lives, health, and prosperity. I am the happiest I have been in my adult life, and I am living life to its fullest.

The big irony to all this is that my future is in much better shape even though I focus most of my attention on the present. By accepting my present reality and seeing it as enjoyable, my creativity and motivation have been soaring. I am working from a state of joy instead of a feeling of obligation, drudgery, or pure responsibility for something or for someone else.

I do things now because I simply enjoy doing them. I live a new life on my terms. I have actually created the very situation I was hoping the money I earned would grant me. I spend lots of my time working on personal growth, speaking, writing, training, coaching, producing empowerment films, and doing all sorts of interesting life experiences and then sharing what I have experienced and learned with others.

I previously thought to myself, "That would be a truly incredible life for me." Now instead of waiting to get to this point later, I decided to find a way to make it happen right now. I realized that telling myself I would and could do certain things later was just an excuse. Do you ever catch yourself saying, "Someday when I have or do this, I will then do this?"

Deep down, you know that it is fear instead of money that is holding you back. It is just fear or simply failing to choose the time for you. Find a way to do those things right now, if only on a small scale.

Living in the now has produced some amazing results for me. You see, the mind is unable to know if you have millions of dollars in the bank. The mind only knows what you tell it. Start living today as if you have all the riches in the world. Be responsible, and be authentic with your money.

When I win $200 million in the lottery, I will keep doing exactly what I am doing right now. The money will simply expand my capacity to accomplish what I choose to continue doing. Figure out what you are able to do to expand your capacity to accomplish and find a way to begin doing it on some level right now.

Choose to live life right now.

■ ■ ■

Today I am extremely happy. To imagine being this happy on a daily basis five years ago would have been just a dream for me. Now my default emotional state is highly positive. I stopped seeking happiness in the future and instead looked for ways to create it and have it right now. I have noticed the happier I feel, the less attached I am to outcomes. I smile and laugh a lot more, too.

Instead of choosing to acquire money, possessions, or other items, my focus has shifted to self-expression. I have a burning desire to create. One of the great things about focusing on expressing and empowering others instead of acquiring is that I end up accomplishing the very things that enable me to easily acquire whatever I choose. I am simply enjoying and living what I love to do.

How do you feel about your life right at this moment? Are you positive and overflowing with passion? Do you find yourself stuck in the same situation I was in several years ago, sacrificing your present happiness for the hope of a better tomorrow or to enjoy life tomorrow?

How is this strategy working for you? Are you becoming significantly happier and more fulfilled with each passing year? Are you just running on a treadmill while convincing yourself that someday things will be better for you?

Step off the treadmill and into the life you deserve to have. Make the authentic choice for yourself, and start living the life you deserve to right now. Keep the destination in sight, and enjoy the process. Be the Warrior, and choose to live in the here and now.

Are you living in the present moment?

■ ■ ■

WARRIOR ACTION STEPS

■ ■ ■

LIVE IN THE NOW.

Living in the present moment eliminates looking forward to uncertainty or backward to pain and regret.

1. Live in the present moment. Start staying and being in the present moment for at least five minutes a day. It will help remind your consciousness to "stay present." This awareness will then begin to permeate other activities in your life until "staying present" becomes the way to be. Schedule your five minutes now.

2. Reality check. Realize "what is" and "what you are able to change." Surrender to "what is." What are you resisting most in life? Step into a place of acceptance at least once a day and embrace "what is." List three things you are able to accept as "what is."

3. Choose peace. The more you practice finding peace in everyday life, the easier it becomes to find peace in the more challenging moments. Ask yourself, "Am I willing to choose love or peace now?" List three things you are able to find peace with.

4. Be present in your conversations with others. Be aware when you start to drift off to somewhere else in any conversation. When this starts to happen, refocus and BE present with the other person or persons. Your conversations will become more effective and more empowering. Your listening skills will also improve.

5. It is critical to know where you choose to go, and it is equally important to be in the moment and enjoy the process along the way. In the end, you realize that the enjoyment of the process is actually the main point. Keep the destination in sight, and enjoy the process.

■ ■ ■

Be Bold, Be Playful, Be Powerful, and Enjoy Your Great Warrior Adventure!

CHAPTER EIGHTEEN

■　■　■

Warrior Simplicity

Simplicity is about subtracting the obvious and adding the meaningful.

■　■　■

Zen describes a happy person as one who leads a simple and peaceful life. Simplicity is easy to understand, clear, concise, and uncomplicated.

I have learned throughout my life that there have been times of complete simplicity and times of complete complexity. In my personal reflection, I have realized the most happy of times for me were the most simple of times. The more stressful times in my life entailed much more complexity.

The times in my life when I had multiple activities, homes, cars, things, insurance, taxes, registrations, or more of this and more of that—more, more, more—these were the most complicated of times and the most stressful of times for me. By most people's standards, I was living the American dream. Instead, I was living the American nightmare of complexity.

> **Life is really simple. We insist on making it complicated.** —Confucius
>
> ■ ■ ■

Although I had a lot of stuff and was always on the go, my life was complicated and full of unwanted chaos. I felt empty inside. I realized that for me to get back to my true, authentic self and to reclaim my inner playful and powerful Warrior self, I had to get back to the basic fundamentals. I had to simplify.

The more I simplified, the more I felt empowered to enjoy and actually accomplish more. The little things became important. The simplicity of life created a stronger internal creativity. This led to a heightened productivity.

Warriors like things simple and perform at their best when it is simple. Simplicity creates a positive flow. Find your simplicity, and embrace your strength. Simplicity is one of those things many people say they desire. Few actually live with simplicity. In my experience, there are two primary reasons why people tend to overcomplicate things.

The first is a loss of focus. Many people tend to have no plan or direction in where they are going. Many seek *all* the various choices available to them. Where there is choice, there is complexity and misery.

When you lose touch with why you are doing something, what you are doing, and where you are going, or when you begin chasing multiple things, you inadvertently sentence yourself to trivial pursuits and challenges. The next thing you know, you are lost or have created a life of chaos, challenges, and complexity.

A good example of loss of focus is chasing more than one rabbit at a time. You may chase them all; however, you will be unable to catch any of them. It is much easier to have clarity and focus on one.

The key to having focus is having clarity. Where there is clarity, there is no choice. Where there is clarity, there is simplicity. Where there is simplicity, there is power.

The other major reason we flock to complexity is a challenge of a very different nature. This requires a completely different solution. Society has rooted this in the ego. The ego's primary lubricant is summed up in one word: *more*. More stuff, more activities, more things, more money, more, more, more. We have become a "more society."

The perception of the ego is that more is better, big is better than small, and less is just plain worse. More, more, more. This perception and behavior create more complexity and difficulty than required. The ego loves complexity and is induced by fear. Our ego relies on fear to protect itself, and complexity is a great place to hide behind.

The process of reaching an ideal state of simplicity at times may seem to be truly complex for you. The easiest way to achieve simplicity is through thoughtful reduction. When in doubt, just remove. Be sure you are congruent with what you choose to remove or reduce in your life. Warriors love to keep it simple.

Remember the K-I-S-S principle: Keep It Splendidly Simple. It is a mantra that always pops into my head when I'm looking at doing something. How easy is it? How easy is it for me to learn or do? You get the picture.

Keep it clear. Think before you act. Many complications arise because of hasty actions. So before you commit yourself to doing an act, think. Think twice for easier or simple alternatives that lead to the same desired result. Always choose the simplicity. You will have more peace with simplicity.

Simplicity is about subtracting the obvious and adding the meaningful. How do you get rid of all your stuff that means so much and evokes so much emotion? The simplest way to achieve simplicity is through thoughtful reduction.

As you simplify, you will notice the most important things are left. A bunch of stuff. This applies to everyday items, closets, and even many of your sentimental treasures. Oftentimes the most difficult stuff to get rid of is all of the stuff soaked in great memories. When you become attached to things that remind you of your past and your loved ones, these usually fill you with lovely memories. Because you choose to simplify your life from stuff, these treasures are buried in boxes in the garage or attic. They are only rediscovered during a move or a special trip down memory lane.

After a recent move I experienced, I realized there were several ways to simplify all these sentimental items. I started focusing on what was most important to me, and I began to honor some of my history. I placed some of my items on display or started using them. The remaining items, I gave away to other family members or donated to charity.

When you come across things that you are unable to use, simply let go of them. Someone else may find your sentimental items to be quite useful. Use them or pass them on. I started to give away many of my items to others who could use what I had. I also realized there are many people in need of the many items I had, so I donated them. One of my friends, Bobby Shirley, said to me, "One man's trash is another man's treasure." I looked at my items as good items, so I decided to share them with others who would embrace them. I actually became excited to see how someone else would enjoy an item I had given away. I felt a strong sense of enjoyment and simple release.

> **Warriors enjoy keeping things simple. The more simple it is, the more Warriors thrive.**
>
> ■ ■ ■

> **Simplicity is the ultimate sophistication.** —Leonardo da Vinci
>
> ■ ■ ■

As you simplify your life, you will come to the realization that the most sentimental things are more than things. They are stories of the people and places you love and about how you spent your time. Write about the things you love instead of holding onto them. Start a family blog or keep a personal journal. Your words may start out describing your grandparents' items and how they were received; your description may turn into a beautiful story about an afternoon the two of you spent together.

Approach each area, and enjoy what unfolds. Clearly identify what is most meaningful to you. Instead of filling boxes with the things that define your life, spend more time creating your life, giving to others, and sharing your story with thoughts, actions, and gratitude.

To keep things simple, regularly ask yourself this question: "Is this making my life easier and more simple?" Creating simplicity in your life will create a much more focused, powerful, and fun life. Reclaim your fun and playful side. Enjoy and simplify your life.

What do you have in your life that you may reduce out of your life right now to make your life more simple?

■ ■ ■

WARRIOR ACTION STEPS

■ ■ ■

SIMPLICITY

**As you simplify your life, the laws
of the universe will be simpler.**

1. Always ask yourself this question: "Is this making
   things easier and more simple for me?" List three
   things you are able to do to make things easier
   for yourself.

2. Your commitments and responsibilities.

   a. Create a list of all your commitments in your life,
      both personal and professional. Include hobbies,
      clubs, online groups, civic groups, your kids' activi-
      ties, sports, home stuff, and so forth—anything
      that regularly requires your time.

   b. Now pick out the few of those that provide you
      value, enjoyment, and long-term benefits.

   c. Toss the rest, if possible. This will provide you with
      a life that has the commitments you enjoy and
      choose to accept.

3. Four steps of simplicity.

   a. Collect everything in one place.

   b. Choose the essential.

   c. Eliminate the rest.

   d. Organize the remaining items.

■ ■ ■

**Be Bold, Be Playful, Be Powerful, and
Enjoy Your Great Warrior Adventure!**

CHAPTER NINETEEN

■　■　■

Have Fun and Enjoy the Journey

Imagination is a faculty of the mind that can be cultivated, developed, extended, and broadened by use. The world has become accustomed to new discoveries. Go create your discoveries.

■　■　■

An essential part of your Warrior journey, as stated in the Declaration of Independence, is the pursuit of life, liberty, and the pursuit of happiness. Fun, playfulness, and humor is the fabric of happy memories. It is the icing on the cake of life.

You are also responsible for choosing to have fun. Your words mixed with any of your feelings of emotions constitute a "magnetic force" that attracts other similar or related thoughts. How about choosing it to be fun, playful, and enjoyable?

I have learned that when I am having fun in my life, I am more focused, I am more productive, I am more relaxed, and I am more at peace. Having fun for me is essential to the pursuit of my goals, dreams, aspirations, and purpose. Part of my personal purpose is to have fun and enjoy each and every moment of my life.

As I have previously shared, all of my closest friends and associates have said when I am playful I am much more enjoyable to be around. I have definitely realized that my relaxed and playful side is what most people enjoy from me. As I become more playful, I become more powerful. I am able to move people into positive action—all because of my own playfulness, which creates positive energy and flow. The more I smile, the more I have impact. Simply being playful and smiling creates a positive, powerful action for me and for others.

> ## Have fun, be playful, and live your life to the fullest.
>
> ■ ■ ■

Have fun and be playful. Use your humor to place a smile on someone else's face as well as your own. Fun, playfulness, and humor are all key to having and maintaining good health for yourself. Being fun, playful, and humorous is also a key to your longevity. It adds years to your life and life to your years. Choose to love life, laugh a lot, and live longer.

You are the architect. Be the architect of a fun, playful, and humorous one. Fun, playfulness, and humor also creates a lighter and more enjoyable experience, especially when it comes to deadlines, chaos, stress, and all of the activities you may live with. Create fun and happiness when you enter a room. The shortest distance between two people is a warm smile and a good laugh. Laughter is an umbilical cord that connects people. It is a lubricant that goes a long way toward building long and fruitful relationships.

The key to creating and maintaining fun, playfulness, and humor is being conscious of choosing to have them as priorities in your life—to embrace and use your fun, playfulness, and humor wherever you go.

Appreciate and celebrate yourself. Choose time to appreciate how far you have come on your journey no matter where you are right now. You have come to this very point. Choose to celebrate doing so. Everything you have experienced in your life's journey has had to happen for you to get to the very place you are right now. So celebrate it.

Start celebrating every step of *your* journey. Celebration is about honoring yourself. It refuels your fire. It soothes your soul, and it feels great. With it, your efforts will keep the wind in your sails. Life is full of big and little opportunities to celebrate. Some would say celebrating and experiencing joy *is* what life is all about. Just start celebrating. Celebrate everything you are able to—birthdays, anniversaries, holidays, and even "ordinary" days.

Give to yourself. Accept that you are able to give to others to the extent you are giving to yourself. When resistance is simply removed from your life, happiness naturally emerges for you. Putting yourself first, having fun, and being playful is being "self-full." Keep your energy vibration high. One of the most effective ways is through daily fun, playfulness, and gratitude.

Now is the time for you to enjoy your journey. A journey where all roads lead to the life you choose. Your life is worth celebrating. Go celebrate it. Have fun, be playful, and smile.

**Are you living a life full of
fun, playfulness, and humor?
How big is your smile?**

■　■　■

WARRIOR ACTION STEPS

■ ■ ■

HAVE FUN AND ENJOY THE PROCESS.

What are you able to celebrate in your life right now?

1. Start celebrating. Celebrate everything you are able to. Ask yourself, "What daily celebration would I like to give special attention to over the coming week?" Name three things you are able to celebrate right now.

2. Keep your energy vibration high. One of the most effective ways is through daily gratitude. Write down at least three things you are grateful for at the end of each day.

3. Continue to document your story daily in your journal.

4. Choose to be happy and have fun. This is your choice. Smile and be warm, friendly, and open. Name three things you are able to smile about right now.

5. Reach out to someone you care about each day, and let that person know how much he or she means to you.

■ ■ ■

Be Bold, Be Playful, Be Powerful, and Enjoy Your Great Warrior Adventure!

CHAPTER TWENTY

■ ■ ■

Leave a Warrior Legacy

There is only one kind of life that truly wins: one that has major impact on others in a positive way.

■ ■ ■

I have personally witnessed the power of leaving a legacy. My parents' current living legacy has shown me how to live a productive and purpose-driven life. They have always encouraged me to be all that I could be and am and to live a life with purpose. Their positive encouragement to be my best and go after what honors me has assisted me in being able to go after my goals, dreams, and aspirations with purpose.

My grandfather, "Pop," left a legacy. He laid out both a financial legacy and one of character. The financial side is an obvious one. More importantly, he left a legacy built upon solid character principles. An important thing I also learned from him was that you are able to plan for tomorrow; however, you have to live in the here and now. I learned that what you do right now will have an impact both now and in the future. He shared these principles with me when I was a small boy, and they have been with me ever since.

Another great legacy I have witnessed firsthand is the one of Coach John Wooden's. He had a huge impact on the players he coached, the coaches he taught, and the university where he coached at, UCLA. He has had a huge impact on this nation. As I previously shared, I had the distinct pleasure of meeting and learning from Coach Wooden. He was the mentor of mentors, and he created the "Pyramid of Success," which is a core philosophy of competitive sports as well as life. It is a legacy in itself.

Coach Wooden shared this:

> Everything in the world is passed down. Every piece of knowledge is something that has been shared by someone else. If you understand it as I do, mentoring becomes your true legacy. It is the greatest inheritance you can give to others. It is why you get up every day: to teach and be taught.

The last time I saw Coach Wooden, I told him I would do my part to carry on his legacy with what he had taught me.

I have personally seen how these legacies have had an impact on so many. My parents, grandparents, and Coach Wooden showed me how having and leaving a legacy is truly important.

You will leave a legacy, too. The question is, "What will my legacy be?" Purposeful living is the foundation of leaving a legacy, a life well lived. Have you ever thought about how your life will affect others long after you have left this earth?

> **To the world you are just one person.**
> **To one person you may be the world.**
>
> ■ ■ ■

For centuries, Warriors have left legacies for others to follow. Think about those who left a legacy for you to follow.

These are the people you have known and who have shaped you deeply:

- Your parents
- Your grandparents
- Your aunts and uncles
- Your schoolteachers
- Your coaches
- Your neighbors where you grew up

A legacy will be either negative or positive. It all depends on how you choose to live your life. Leaving a legacy for others to follow is part of what drives me daily. I follow others who have gone before me. They left a legacy for me. Now I am consciously choosing to create a legacy for those who come after me so they will have a trail to follow as well. You see, leaving a legacy is important.

Why is leaving a legacy important? Here are a few reasons. The legacy you leave is part of the ongoing foundations of life. Those who came before you left you the world you live in. Those who will come after will have only what you leave them. You are a steward of this world, and you have a calling to leave it better than you found it.

How you live your life is critically important. I challenge you to evaluate how you live. I challenge you to think deeply about the major areas of your life where you are able to leave a lasting legacy.

There are literally thousands of men and women who have lived in ways that affect your life today. Legacies have raw power. There are people who have changed the world for good, people who have opened up new worlds for millions of others, and people who have spurred others on to new heights.

There are also people who have been responsible for and caused massive destruction for countless millions—people who left a wake of pain behind them wherever they went. There are parents who have blessed their children with greatness and other parents who have ruined their children's fragile minds and hearts.

> **Purposefully leaving a legacy for others creates a life of self-fullness.**
>
> ■ ■ ■

Leaving a legacy is an act of responsibility. Living a life with your purpose is the best way to leave a positive and powerful legacy. When you start with the end in mind, you have a personal direction to guide all of your activities. Beginning with the end in mind is choosing control of your own life and giving meaning to the actions you choose every day.

Start building a vision for your life. Imagine it is your 100th birthday. What would you like to have achieved with your life by then? When you understand the legacy you choose to leave behind, you will gain clarity on your life's purpose. A legacy is simply the captured summary of your life's purpose *achieved*. What you do affects others. Your life has the power to create what you choose to have. Live and do great things with it.

Because of the power of your life and the legacy you leave, it is a great responsibility to choose to leave a positive legacy. All Warriors choose to create legacies that will enable the next generation. I truly believe part of what makes us rise up to be a honorable Warrior is having a foundational part of our lives based on the goal of leaving a legacy. What is your legacy? What does your legacy say about you?

Purposefully leaving a legacy for others breaks the downward pull of selfishness that is inherent in you. *It creates a life of self-fullness.* When you strive to leave a legacy, you are acting with a selflessness that will be good for you and others.

> **Building a legacy that will last beyond your life is purposeful, selfless, and self-full.**
>
> ■ ■ ■

Legacies make life better for those who come after you, aside from your own wealth, fame, or recognition. Leaving a legacy is about helping others. Building a legacy that will last beyond your life is purposeful, selfless, and self-full.

Living with that thought in mind breaks the power of selfishness. It ingrains itself in your life. It also keeps you focused on the big picture. Legacy building is "big picture" living. It keeps you focused on the long term and gives you values through which you choose your actions. When you build a life that will give for many years to come, you are living with a daily purpose.

Uncover what truly drives you. Recognize your inherent strengths, embrace them, and share them with the world. Develop a greater understanding of others, and pay it forward. Welcome home, Warrior. Enjoy your playful and powerful Warrior legacy.

How is your legacy going to have an impact on others?

■ ■ ■

WARRIOR ACTION STEPS

■ ■ ■

LEAVE A WARRIOR LEGACY

To achieve greatness, one must be dedicated to the journey. Live your life with the end in mind.

1. Your legacy is very important.

    a. Are you celebrating your life? Start celebrating and continue celebrating your life.

    b. Reflect today on how you are going to build a life that leaves a tremendous legacy.

    c. Ask yourself: "How does this action affect my overall purpose?"

    d. Ask yourself: "How will this affect people in the years to come?"

2. What is your "why"? Write out clearly what your "why" for leaving a legacy is.

3. Look carefully at the people around you. What difference would you like to have made in their lives? Choose action today and do it.

4. Choose a time to imagine how your legacy will positively affect others. What are three things you choose to do in creating your extraordinary legacy?

5. What is your legacy going to be? Clearly write out what your purpose in life is and how your legacy is going to be from this moment forward. Does your purpose line up with your legacy? Do you require making any adjustments? If so, what?

■ ■ ■

Be Bold, Be Playful, Be Powerful, and Enjoy Your Great Warrior Adventure!

CHAPTER TWENTY-ONE

■ ■ ■

Being the Playful and Powerful Warrior You Are

He who has a why to live, will bear almost any how.

■ ■ ■

Wherever you are is simply a new starting point. Upon reflection, I realize that I wasted blocks of my life. You may run or dance as fast as you are able to, distracting yourself from the inner work that you require for yourself, and ultimately, all this activity will do is falsely fill a void for you. To increase inner peace, you must find the courage to examine and embrace all aspects of yourself—the positive, the negative, the light, the dark, the happy, the sad, the new, and the old.

You are closer to realizing and having all of your goals, dreams, and aspirations. Find the love, peace, playfulness, and power inside of you to live a meaningful life on purpose, with purpose, and for purpose. Apply what you have learned in this book, and start your new Warrior journey now. Right here and right now.

Now it is decision time. What do you choose for yourself? What are you going to do with the remaining blocks of your life? Be the great Warrior adventurer. Be the great Warrior you are. Enjoy the rest of your playful and powerful Warrior life.

The Playful and Powerful Warrior Principles

1. Place God first.
2. Enjoy the great adventure of your Warrior journey.
3. Be playful.
4. Be powerful.
5. Find and live your purpose.
6. Know your "why."
7. Be purposeful. Design your purpose into your everyday life.
8. Forgive yourself and others.
9. Always come from love.
10. Understand and watch your ego.
11. Understand what you control. You control your thoughts, words, and actions.
12. Be aware of your conscious language, and choose adjustments when necessary.
13. Understand the power of your thoughts, words, and actions.
14. Know if and when to be on someone else's stage.
15. Be authentic; live authentically.
16. Always come from your best.
17. Embrace your magnificence and Warrior greatness.
18. Surround yourself with the right people.
19. Have big, big goals, dreams, and aspirations.
20. Use positive, action-oriented thoughts and words to manifest your goals, dreams, and aspirations.
21. Live and be in the now.
22. Listen to your inner voice.
23. Have courage and use it daily to live.
24. Be simple; live simply.
25. Have belief.
26. Have fun and enjoy the process.
27. Share your story.
28. Leave a Warrior legacy.
29. Be bold.
30. Choose action now.

Be Bold, Be Playful, Be Powerful, and Enjoy Your Great Warrior Adventure!

■ ■ ■

ACKNOWLEDGMENTS

■ ■ ■

**The most important investment
you will ever make is in YOU.**

■ ■ ■

I have had many great teachers. There are too many to list. Below are some of the ones who have had a distinct impact on me and who also inspired the desire to write this book.

I thank Coach Dale Brown. He has been a coach, teacher, mentor, and most importantly, one of my closest friends. Thanks, Coach.

Coach Brown introduced me to Coach Wooden. I have read and listened to everything Coach Wooden has written and taught. Thank you, Coach Wooden, for sharing, and you are missed. As I shared with Coach Wooden in 2008, I will do my part to carry your legacy forward. Thank you, Coach.

I thank my mom and dad, Nancy and Gary, and both sets of my grandparents, Nana and Pop, and Mimi and Papa. All of their love, support, and encouragement showed me how I could be all that I could be—and am. They all said that someday they would write a book, and I would, too. On behalf of them, I am part of that process. Thank you all.

I thank John MacNaught for lessons I learned from him when I was a young man. He showed me (without even knowing it) that writing is a great form of expression for me. I also learned many other lessons from him about sales, marketing, entrepreneurism, and hockey. Thanks, John.

I thank Greg Klein for his love, encouragement, and wisdom. He assisted me in learning how to see differently, choose again, and apply choices in my life. Greg also shared a simple and powerful analogy about getting on or being on someone's stage—only when invited. Thank you, Greg.

> **When you desire something enough, you will find the willpower to achieve it.**
>
> ■ ■ ■

I thank Jerry Medol, who showed me how to channel my own hurts, anger, and feelings into positive releases. He taught me how any feeling, good or bad, was okay to embrace, accept, and release. He also shared with me how the mind is unable to know the difference between whether something has actually happened or only a thought within the mind. Thanks, Jerry.

I thank my good friend Michael Accurso. Michael said many times, "G, you need to tell your story. You will have an impact on millions of people." Michael encouraged me to embrace my past situation, when I almost made the choice to take my own life. He insisted, "People out in the world right now can identify with your story, and it will assist them in their healing or in their wanting to strive for more." Michael, thanks for your openness, honesty, discernment, and encouragement to write this book.

I thank Alita Maye. You have provided great support and authentic friendship. I appreciate the honesty and patience you have displayed with me. I thank you for your insight and your assistance with this book, which is now completed because of you. Thank you.

I thank three young entrepreneurs, Ryan Blair, Nick Sarnicola, and Blake Mallen. I have had the pleasure of coaching, consulting, mentoring, and partnering with these men. More importantly, they have all had a distinct impact in my life through their coaching and mentoring me as well. Thank you for inspiring me and assisting me in reigniting the fire within me. You have shown me that mentorship and leadership may be accomplished, regardless of any age differences or experience levels. All three of you are my younger brothers. Just a little bit younger, though.

I thank ViSalus Sciences and the Body by Vi 90-Day Challenge for showing me how I could become healthy and physically fit as a Warrior. ViSalus has allowed me the time and freedom to write this book.

I thank my original Fusion Certified Trainers (FCTs), Jake Trzcinski, Jason Lew, and Pete and Nicole Bunting, for all your encouragement and friendship.

I thank a team of people whose positive actions in building our business have allowed me to choose the time to write this book: Eric Hill, Mike and Lavon Craig, Kyle and Susan Pacetti, Robby Long, Dale and Linda Croy, Ethan Lanagan, Jason and Amber Silverthorn, Rich Pala, Jeremy Gilchrist, Vicky Meyer, Bridget Reid, Scott and Shanda Whitney, Paul and Mysti Wehrum, Tim and Holly Kirkland, Ashley Riggs, Michael Reynolds, James Reynolds, Alita Armknecht, Christine Culling, Dr. Pamela Green, Clive and Gaudia Aquart, Bill Nissen, Bryan and Brandi Bellville, Neil Bellville, Tina Hicks, Hazen Christensen, Christy and Brannon East, Tony and Rhonda Lucero, Alex Bonds, Greg Culpepper, Ginger Hall, Kevin Sergent, Melissa Howard, Phil Watson, Sarah Glazer, Matt Ward, Shae Adams, Jon Harkness, Brian Cummings, Ali Sharareh, Lester Earl, Mel Cerveny, John Laun, Zorica Bosev, Noreen Otey, John Tolmie, John Purdy,

Audrey Sommerfeld, Dr. Michael Seidman, Jennifer Golevski, and Joe Perez. I have also learned many lessons about myself from each of you. Thank you.

I thank all my fellow Beach Buddies of BeachLifestyle.com who have shown me how to live as a Warrior, BeachLifestyle.

I thank the following team of people who have been instrumental in assisting me in completing this book: Erica Jennings, Judith Emmert, Deanne Lachner, Alita Armknecht, Nancy Reynolds, Greg Klein, Mel Cerveny, Blake Mallen, Janet Kelly, Forbes Riley, Shae Adams, Larry Carpenter, Jon MacVarish, Dale Brown, and Eric Hill. Thank you all.

I thank Oprah Winfrey for inspiring me to share my experiences to assist others to transform their lives. Thank you for also sharing one powerful statement: "Find your flow and go with the current of your life." I have and I am. Thank you.

I thank Gary Novotny and Nate Rutt at Gary Michaels Clothiers for their ability to provide high-quality and fashionable clothing to dress like a Warrior. Thank you.

Finally, I thank all of the many lessons I have had from *all* of the people I have come in contact with during my lifetime. I have been truly blessed by each and every one. You all have made a lasting and positive impact on me. Thank you all.

**You design your future.
Find your flow and go with
the current of your life.**

■ ■ ■

ABOUT THE AUTHOR

■ ■ ■

I am a playful and powerful Warrior.

■ ■ ■

G J Reynolds, also known as "G," is a passionate entrepreneur, business developer, trainer, public speaker, and author who thrives on teaching people how to improve their lives.

Ten years ago, it was a different story. Reynolds was 40 years old and living the American dream as a successful business owner. He enjoyed the thrill of accumulating "things" and the attention that came along with it. Despite having material success, Reynolds craved more. As he says, "I had a lot of stuff!" He eventually became deeply depressed and suicidal.

"While others saw greatness and accomplishment, I saw a sellout. While others saw success, I saw failure. Externally, I looked great. Internally I was a feeling like a complete mess," says Reynolds. "I began to wonder how I could have so much and be so empty. I had spent the better part of my adulthood chasing the external world and ignoring *living* within my internal world."

Upon hitting rock bottom in 2001, Reynolds had a vision: God led him out of the darkness saying, "You do *not* have a reason die. You have a reason to *live*. I will show you how."

Today, Reynolds's mission is teaching people how to elevate their lives. For the first time, he shares his inspiring story in *The Playful and Powerful Warrior within YOU! How to Reclaim Your Personal Power and Live a Fulfilling Life of True Adventure.* With the book, he hopes to evoke lasting life changes, bringing readers one step closer to their dreams and own empowerment.

Reynolds spent five years in the U.S. Army as a satellite communications specialist, achieving the rank of sergeant. He graduated from MidAmerica Nazarene University with a bachelor of arts in management of human resources and then spent five years in the corporate world as a telecommunications specialist and manager. All three companies he worked for in the telecommunications industry were acquired and/or merged to become Verizon.

In 1991, Reynolds became an entrepreneur and has since owned or operated several successful telecommunications and business marketing and development companies. Reynolds has assembled and trained sales and marketing teams of over 50,000. He specializes in working with like-minded entrepreneurs and professionals who choose to raise the bar for themselves and their businesses.

G is on a mission to assist millions of people to transform their lives. Need a little help?

To contact GJ Reynolds, visit www.simplyg.net

I BELIEVE IN YOU.

■ ■ ■

MISSION G

■ ■ ■

**Effective receiving is reciprocated
by open giving.** —Mother Teresa

■ ■ ■

Ten percent of every book sale is donated to Mission G. Your generosity will help shape the future of communities across the world.

Mission G is an organization created to assist others to enhance their life, health, and prosperity. Mission G focuses on uniting talented and passionate leaders around a worthwhile cause of enriching people's lives.

Mission G focuses on providing underprivileged children with education and health. Mission G also works with Feed The Children, an initiative that provides nutritional meals to underprivileged children.

Mission G also assists Project NOW (Nurturing of Our Warriors), which helps former military personnel with the transition from active duty to being and living productive lives as a civilians.

**To donate, please go to
www.missiong.org**

■ ■ ■

More Resources from PowerfulWarrior.com

■ ■ ■

THE WARRIOR WAY
The Playful & Powerful Warrior Handbook

Your responsibility is to honor being the best you are—your true, authentic self. This handbook provides you the opportunity to apply the principles you have learned and create a plan to achieve your goals.

It is your step-by-step guide to reclaiming your personal power and living a fulfilling life of true adventure. This handbook is an essential tool for further experiencing and processing what you have learned from the *Playful and Powerful Warrior within YOU!*

To order additional copies of *The Playful and Powerful Warrior within YOU!* and to download *The Warrior Way* e-book, visit

www.PowerfulWarrior.com

■ ■ ■

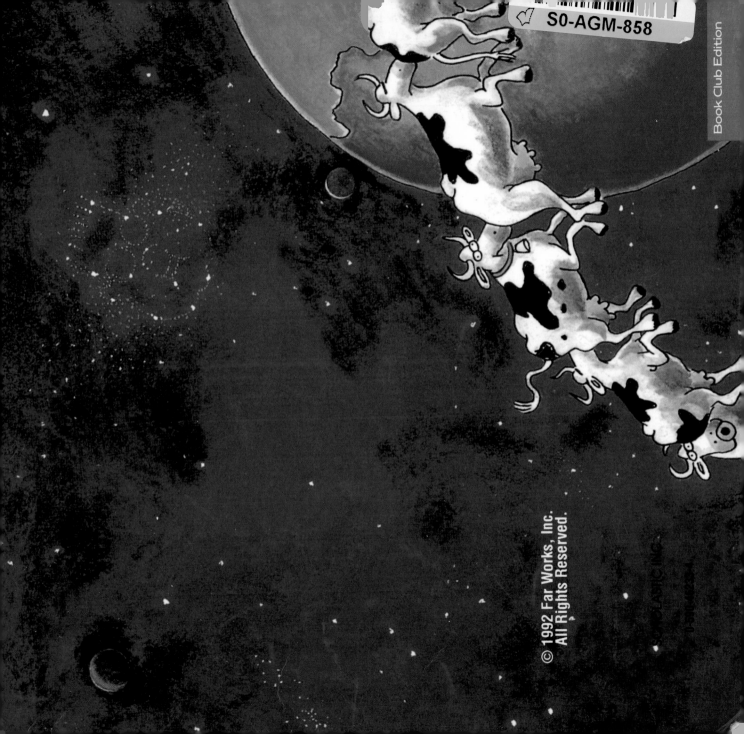

COWS of OUR PLANET

A Far Side
collection

Other Books in The Far Side Series

The Far Side
Beyond The Far Side
In Search of The Far Side
Bride of The Far Side
Valley of The Far Side
It Came From The Far Side
Hound of The Far Side
The Far Side Observer
Night of the Crash-Test Dummies
Wildlife Preserves
Wiener Dog Art
Unnatural Selections

Anthologies

The Far Side Gallery
The Far Side Gallery 2
The Far Side Gallery 3

Retrospective

The PreHistory of The Far Side: A 10th Anniversary Exhibit

COWS of OUR PLANET

A Far Side
collection
by

Gary Larson

SCHOLASTIC INC.
New York Toronto London Auckland Sydney

The Far Side is distributed internationally by Universal Press Syndicate.

Printed on recycled paper.

ISBN 0-590-46233-4

12 11 10 9 8 7 6 5 4 3 2 1   3 4 5 6 7 8/9

Printed in the U.S.A.   02

First Scholastic printing, January 1993

"Hey . . . this could be the chief."

Colonel Sanders at the Pearly Gates

While their owners sleep, nervous
little dogs prepare for their day.

6

Three more careers are claimed by
the Bermuda Triangle of jazz.

The life and times of Lulu, Mrs. O'Leary's ill-fated cow

7

The herd moved in around him, but Zach had known better than to approach these animals without his trusty buffalo gum.

Basic lives

"Margaret! You? . . . I . . . I . . . should . . . have . . . knowwwwwwnnnnn . . ."

Unbeknownst to most ornithologists, the dodo was actually a very advanced species, living alone quite peacefully until, in the 17th century, it was annihilated by men, rats, and dogs. As usual.

Unwittingly, Raymond wanders into the hive's company picnic.

"Look. We know *how* you did it — *how* is no longer the question. What we now want to know is *why*. . . . Why now, brown cow?"

And then Al realized his problems were much bigger than just a smashed truck.

"I tell ya, Ben — no matter who wins this thing,
Boot Hill ain't ever gonna be the same."

"OK, McFadden. . . . So *that's* the way you wanna play."

Modern art critic

Every afternoon a sugar cube dealer would slowly
cruise the corral looking for "customers."

"Man, the Kellermans are bold! . . . If it wasn't for our screens, they'd probably walk right in!"

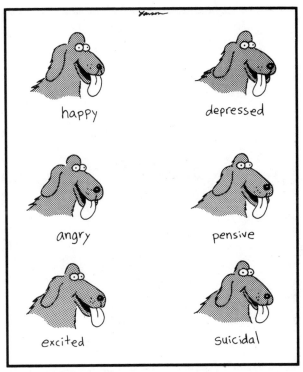

How to recognize the moods of an Irish setter

"Well, first the bad news — you're definitely hooked."

Tomorrow, they would be mortal enemies. But on the eve of the great
hunt, feelings were put aside for the traditional Mammoth Dance.

The action suddenly stopped while both sides waited
patiently for the hornet to calm down.

Eventually, Billy came to dread his father's lectures
over all other forms of punishment.

On the air with "Snake Talk"

"Lord, we thank thee."

Vera looked around the room. Not another
chicken anywhere. And then it struck her —
this was a hay bar.

Junior high gorillas

For many weeks, the two species had lived in mutual tolerance of one another. And then, without provocation, the hornets began throwing rocks at Ned's house.

Abraham Lincoln's first car

The nightly crisis of Todd's stomach vs.
Todd's imagination

Centaur rodeos

How poodles first came to North America

Suddenly, Fish and Wildlife agents burst in on
Mark Trail's poaching operation.

The first Dirt Capades

"Look here, McGinnis — hundreds of bright copper kettles, warm woolen mittens, brown paper packages tied up with string. . . . Someone was after a few of this guy's favorite things."

The life and times of baby Jessica

High above the hushed crowd, Rex tried to remain focused. Still, he couldn't shake one nagging thought: He was an old dog and this was a new trick.

Hell's video store

Custer's recurrent nightmare

"Same as the others, O'Neill. The flippers, the
fishbowl, the frog, the lights, the armor. . . .
Just one question remains: Is this the work
of our guy, or a copycat?"

Sumo temporaries

"Well, there he goes again. . . . I suppose I shouldn't worry, but I just get a bad feeling about Jimmy hanging with those tuna punks."

Fortunately for Sparky, Zeke knew the famous "Rex maneuver."

Henry never knew what hit him.

"And so please welcome one of this cartoon's most esteemed scientist-like characters, Professor Boris Needleman, here to present his paper, 'Beyond the Border: Analysis, Statistical Probability, and Speculation of the Existence of Other Cartoons on the Known Comics Page.'"

Fly dates

"Well, we're ready for the males' 100-meter freestyle, and I think we can rest assured that most of these athletes will select the dog paddle."

Shoot!.. I'm gonna go back and try this again.

At the monthly meeting of Squidheads Anonymous

In what was destined to be a short-lived spectacle,
a chicken, suspended by a balloon, floated through
the Samurai bar's doorway.

Carl "Javahead" Jones and his
chopped espresso maker

"Curse you, Flannegan! Curse you to *hell*! . . . there, I've said it."

"Voila! . . . Your new dream home! If you like it,
I can get a crew mixing wood fibers and saliva
as early as tomorrow."

"Oh, my God, Rogers! . . . Is that? . . . Is that?
It is! It's the *mummy's purse!*"

"According to these figures, Simmons, your
department has lost another No. 2 Double A,
and I want you to find it!"

"Give me a hand here, boys! It's young Will Hawkins!
. . . Dang fool tried to ride into the sunset!"

Charlie Brown in Indian country

"You gotta help me, Mom. . . . This assignment is
due tomorrow, and Gramps doesn't
understand the new tricks."

Carl had never had so much fun in his whole life, and he knew, from this moment on, that he would never again be a lone pine tree.

Professor Glickman, the lab practical joker, deftly
places a single drop of hydrochloric acid on
the back of Professor Bingham's neck.

Mike Wallace interviews the Devil.

Social morays

That night, their revenge was meted out on both
Farmer O'Malley and his wife. The next day,
police investigators found a scene that they could
describe only as "grisly, yet strangely hilarious."

Stumpy didn't know how he got in this situation,
but with the whole town watching, he knew
he'd have to play it out.

Roommates Elvis and Salman Rushdie sneak a
quick look at the outside world.

Donning his new canine decoder, Professor Schwartzman becomes the first human being on Earth to hear what barking dogs are actually saying.

"You're a long way from Big Poodle, stranger. . . .
This here is Dead Skunk, and if I were you
I'd just keep on movin'."

"Why don't you play some blues, Andrew?"

46

"New guy, huh? Well, up here, you walk the *edge*! And the edge is a fickle hellcat. . . . Love her, but never trust her, for her heart is full of *lye*!"

God at His computer

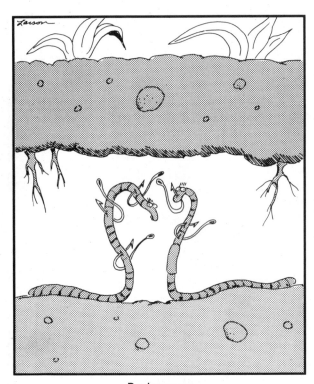

Punk worms

By blending in with the ostrich's eggs, Hare Krishnas
are subsequently raised by the adult birds.

Idaho latrine stalker
(venomous)

Blue-faced stampede agitator
(usually shot by ranchers)

Arkansas baby stomper

Parasitic charolais

Skyscraper suckerfoot

Norwegian one-eyed smiler

Brahma belly

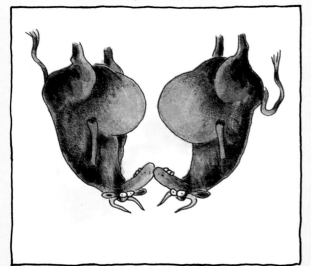

Flying guernsey

Mad scientist hybrid
(happened only once, in the '50s)

Texas longnose
(recently extinct: certain cultures
thought the nose was an aphrodisiac)

Polynesian puffer cow

Toy angus
(extinct)

COWS of OUR PLANET

Larson

New Zealand portaford

Tennessee big butt

Australian spotted roller

Wild highlander
(extinct: couldn't hold their milk)

Golden spitter

Cow mimics

Madagascar tree hereford
(despised by natives
walking below)

Urban street hereford
(rarely seen)

Three Mile Island guernsey
(North American cousin to
the Chernobyl angus)

Western skipper

Amazon river cow

"Bad guy comin' in, Arnie! . . . Minor key!"

"Whoa! Mr. Lewis! We don't know what that thing is
or where it came from, but after what happened to
the dog last week, we advise people not to touch it."

Special commuter lanes

Dog ventriloquists

"Yeah, Vern! You heard what I said! And what are you gonna do about it? Huh? C'mon! What are ya gonna do? Huh? *C'mon!*"

"Hey! I got news for you, sweetheart! . . .
I *am* the lowest form of life on earth!"

The art of conversation

Sheep that pass in the night

"I hate 'em. They mess on the stools, they attack the mirror — and, of course, they drink like birds."

"Whoa! Whoa! C'mon, you guys! This is just a friendly game of cards — ease up on those acid-filled beakers."

Of course, prehistoric neighborhoods always had
that one family whose front yard was strewn
with old mammoth remains.

". . . And please let Mom, Dad, Rex, Ginger, Tucker,
me, and all the rest of the family see color."

"Oooo

"I wouldn't do that, bartender. . . . Unless, of course,
you think you're fast enough."

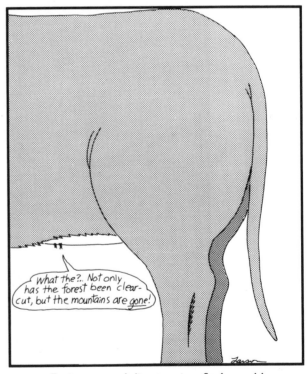

Environmental disasters in a flea's world

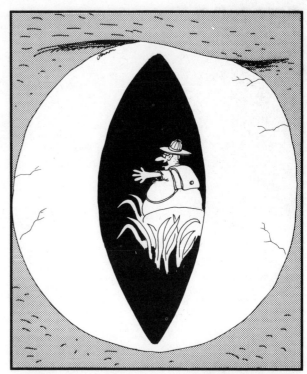

"My gun, Desmond! I sense this striped man-eater is somewhere dead ahead, waiting to ambush us! Ohhhhhh, he thinks he's so clever."

The Blob family at home

"Bob! There's a fly on your lip! . . . There he goes. . . .
He's back! He's back!"

Boid watching

Where the deer and the antelope work

"And now the weather — well, doggone it, but I'm afraid that cold front I told you about yesterday is just baaarrreeely going to miss us."

In the corridors of Clowngress

"Come with us, ma'am — and if I were you, I'd get a good lawyer. No one's gonna buy that my-husband-was-only-hibernating story."

Slave-ship entertainers

"Oh, yeah? Well, I'd rather be a living corpse made from dismembered body parts than a hunchbacked little grave robber like you!"

Giorgio Armani at home

Everything was starting to come into focus for Farmer MacDougal — his missing sheep, his missing beer, and his collie, Shep, who was getting just a little too sociable for his own good.

Early checkers

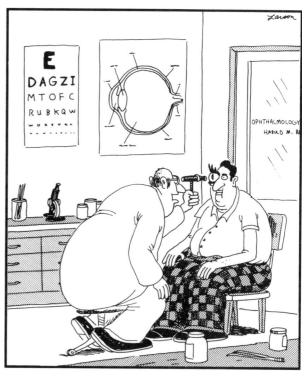

"Oh, this is wonderful, Mr. Gruenfeld — I've only seen it a couple of times. You have corneal corruption. . . . Evil eye, Mr. Gruenfeld, evil eye."

While vacationing in Africa, Pinocchio has his longtime wish to be a real boy suddenly and unexpectedly granted.

Dance of the Beekeepers

Practical jokes of the Paleolithic

"We don't kno...
a disgru...

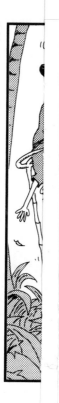

"Well, here we are, my little chickadee."

Acts of God

75

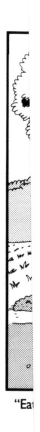

"Eat

> *I wonder if I should put a "happy face" on the uvula.*

God do

Some of our more common "rescue" animals

> *Damn.*

RINGGGGGGG

"Well, time for our weekly
brain-stem-storming session."

"So please welcome our keynote speaker,
Professor Melvin Fenwick — the man who,
back in 1952, first coined the now common phrase:
'Fools! I'll destroy them all!'"

House Beautiful

Bedrooms

House Beautiful

Bedrooms

THE EDITORS OF HOUSE BEAUTIFUL MAGAZINE

TEXT BY
CARA GREENBERG

HEARST BOOKS

A DIVISION OF

STERLING PUBLISHING CO., INC.

NEW YORK

Edited by Laurie Orseck
Interior design by Nancy Steiny Design
Cover design by Deborah Kerner, Dancing Bears Design

Produced by Smallwood & Stewart Inc., New York City

Library of Congress Cataloging-in-Publication Data
Available upon request.

10   9   8   7   6   5   4   3   2   1

First Paperback Edition 2003
Published by Hearst Books
A Division of Sterling Publishing Co., Inc.
387 Park Avenue South, New York, NY 10016

House Beautiful and Hearst Books are trademarks owned by
Hearst Magazines Property, Inc., in USA, and Hearst Communications, Inc., in Canada.

www.housebeautiful.com

Distributed in Canada by Sterling Publishing
^{c}/o Canadian Manda Group, One Atlantic Avenue, Suite 105
Toronto, Ontario, Canada M6K 3E7
Distributed in Australia by Capricorn Link (Australia) Pty. Ltd.
P.O. Box 704, Windsor, NSW 2756 Australia

Printed in China

ISBN 1-58816-228-1

Contents

Introduction

To the long list of things we take for granted these days, let us add the bedroom. It wasn't very long ago that separate chambers for sleeping were unheard of, and privacy for the individual was a completely foreign notion. In medieval Europe, whole families slept in the same hall-like room used for cooking, eating, and even sheltering animals. In the seventeenth and eighteenth centuries, to escape the hubbub in the main hall, some clever, well-to-do individuals conceived the idea of separate rooms for sleeping. By the mid-nineteenth century, bedrooms were commonplace throughout the Western world.

Yet in our fast-paced society, private time and space still seem elusive. The bedroom is more important than ever as a retreat, not just from the more public parts of the house, but from the chaotic world outside. With this primary purpose in mind, the decoration of a bedroom becomes a challenge of the most pleasant sort. The exact forms this may take vary widely ~ from lavish to spare, from traditional to idiosyncratic.

House Beautiful Bedrooms offers abundant proof that decorating the bedroom can inspire great flights of imagination. The boundaries of what is "permissible" have become wider and more expansive than ever, as we draw our inspiration from diverse cultures and the entire history of design.

On the pages that follow, you will find much of what you need to know to create the bedroom of your dreams. But we also hope you will enjoy simply perusing these beautiful rooms, and that you will begin to see their design possibilities in a new, more brilliant light.

Setting a Mood

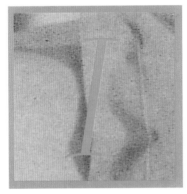

n the geography of a house, the bedroom is the most private sanctuary, a place blessedly free from the public eye. The very appeal of a bedroom is that it is one's own, a place to go and close the door on the world. It is only natural that it is our most personal expression, the most self-indulgent of rooms.

Many people would say a bedroom should be restful, in keeping with its primary function, or perhaps romantic ~ billowing curtains, soft rugs, subtle lighting. But not everyone feels that way. "The bedroom should be as exciting and stimulating as any other room," says one designer, who uses lively colors, bold furnishings, and busy fabrics to implement her vision. "Cheerful by day, sultry by night," says a woman who, confined to her bedroom for months during a difficult pregnancy, chose a metallic wallpaper that metamorphoses by the hour with the changing light.

Whether the ultimate effect is clarity and calm, or a more energetic state of being; whether the desired feeling is historic or of the moment, sophisticated or rustic ~ the bedroom can truly be the stuff of dreams.

SERENE RETREAT

Two hundred years ago, a bedroom was called a cabinet, and it was often just that: an alcove in the wall, with panel doors that could be pulled shut for privacy.

"That's exactly what I wanted ~ a real getaway," says Spruce Roden, a New York City floral designer, of the master bedroom in his Connecticut country house, a central-chimney colonial dating from 1788. The decor was inspired even more specifically by a suite of Federal-period rooms at the Brooklyn Museum in New York City; Roden loved their clean lines, spare furnishings, and palette limited to just two colors. He captured that serene mood by designing a gleaming, snug, wood-sheathed box that gives its inhabitants the illusion of being totally removed from the workaday world.

The house, though old, was not historically important. "It had been messed up so many times, it gave me a certain freedom to mess it up my own way," Roden jokes. But he did make an effort to be true to the Federal period by restoring architectural details that had been stripped away during several zealous renovations. In the master bedroom, the walls were clad in raised pine paneling custom-made in the style of the eighteenth century, then painted a luscious blue-green. New closets, lined in cedar, are hidden behind doors covered with matching panels, which unify the room's perimeter and complete the effect of an

The lush romantic painting above the bed ~ a landscape coincidentally dated 1788, the same year the house was built ~ serves as decorative headboard and also keynote for the color of the walls, a true-to-period blue-green. Creamy linen sheets add to the restfulness and tranquility of the room.

enclosed "cabinet." Many of the furnishings and fabrics are true to the period, including a cherry four-poster bed.

Roden's masterstroke, lending distinction and a certain dressiness to the space, is the coffered ceiling, crafted by a local shipbuilder. The original beams, ravaged by age, were encased in pine boards, then painted glossy white. The result is a comforting space, far removed from the demands of the twentieth century.

Wool damask, the fabric of choice in fine Federal homes, is used for the sofa, draperies, and bedspread. An acorn-and-oak-leaf pattern echoes the acorn motif found on the four-poster's finials. The gold-trimmed sofa, a 1920s copy of a piece found in England's Knole castle, sits in front of a small French Directoire table. Both face a fireplace ~ a luxury on winter nights. The brass wall sconces are modern copies of a period design.

A ROOM WITH TWO VIEWS

The drama inherent in this Manhattan bedroom comes from the dynamic interplay of opposing energies. Owners Katie Ridder, a designer with a fondness for the decorative objects of the Middle East, and her husband, architect Peter Pennoyer, like things crisp and clean ~ and rich and sultry at the same time. The bed's white sheets, and the snappy blue and white striped curtains, for example, could belong to a beach house, while the richly colored folding screen and the arabesque-patterned wallpaper are evocative of a Turkish bazaar.

It is in fact the wallpaper that ties the room's two "personalities" together, literally reversing itself and transforming the mood of the room as the hours go by. By day, the walls are bright and reflective, making the room a cheerful afternoon retreat. Come nightfall, by the glow of brass table lamps, the metallic sheen of the paper tones down to matte, and the atmosphere becomes muted, romantic, mysterious.

At night, especially, the room seems removed from the city that surrounds it. "I love bedrooms that take you away from your environment a little bit," Pennoyer says. "The boring thing is to do a bedroom in a modern apartment pure and white." It is more interesting, he points out, to strike a completely different mood from the rooms you encounter on your way there.

The room's approach to color ~ a subtle handling of the three primaries ~ is a daring one. The warmth of the gold wallpaper makes the space seem to glow as if from within. The blue adds a complementary note of coolness. And touches of red in the fabric screen add interest to an otherwise nondescript corner. Ridder had originally chosen a complex-patterned fabric for the curtains, but Pennoyer vetoed it as "too expected." The couple opted instead for the lighter feeling of the blue and white stripe. The overall effect is energetic, eccentric, and offbeat ~ in a thoroughly comfortable, even luxurious, way.

Color, pattern, and time periods are mixed with assurance in this big-city bedroom. An eighteenth-century straight-legged side table in red maple and a brass lamp by early modernist designer

Walter von Nessen share a cozy corner. The headboard and bedskirt sport the same summery blue and white fabric as the curtains. Simple sisal carpeting quietly pulls the room together.

23

A screen made from fabric from a 1920s theater set incorporates the three primary colors that dominate the room's palette (near right). Amid the exuberant pairing of pattern and color in their master bedroom, white bed linens and a white-draped nighttable provide a few oases of calm (far right). A yellow slipcovered vanity chair keeps company with a birch Biedermeier-style dressing table, crafted in Scandinavia in the 1870s (below right).

AUSTERE BEAUTY WITH A PAST

It takes a reverence for the past to appreciate the gentle, evocative beauty of the rather spare guest bedroom in this 1762 clapboard relic of colonial New England. Here, the mood is one of deep repose. "We wanted to keep it tranquil and calm and authentically of the period," says one of the owners. "Nothing glitzy or jarring that would make someone say, 'Yes, they must have redone this place in the late eighties.'"

Carefully edited and composed by master designer John Saladino, the room is as dignified and pure, and as starkly dramatic, as a Quaker meetinghouse. Yet it also radiates great warmth. "I wanted it to glow at night like the inside of an old lantern," says Saladino. And so it does: The desired rich tallow color was achieved in a two-step process. First, solid ochre paint was applied to the walls as a ground. Then, in a paint technique known as sponge-glazing, a warm cognac color was layered over it.

In fact, the walls in the guest bedroom were the only surfaces that were painted. The original paneled door and window moldings were dry-scraped and intentionally left in rough condition. That approach coincided with the owners' treatment of the entire house, which had never been modernized. Over the generations, numerous coats of paint and wallpaper had virtually encrusted every room. Most surfaces were simply hand-stripped, then left alone, resulting in the mottled, corroded look of broken walls unearthed at an archaeological site.

A pair of reproduction Shaker-style cherry wood beds, their canopies undraped, are compatible with the pristine starkness of the space ~ a starkness relieved only by a pair of white heirloom candlewick coverlets crocheted by the grandmother of one of the owners.

The conscious restraint shown in furnishing the room is in deference to the house's age. Citing details such as the original wide panel doors, the elliptical arch of the fireplace, the wonderful patina of the window casing, and the old glass in the panes, Saladino says, "If we had overfurnished it, some of those subtleties would have been lost."

Even without a blaze, the pure lines of the guest bedroom's big working fireplace are a strong focal point in this New England landmark remodeled by John Saladino. Flanking the hearth are a Mission-style oak chair by Stickley Brothers and a genuine Shaker rocker bought at auction. The kilim rug brings out the cinnamon color of the walls.

There was no need
to fake age in this house.
An appreciation of
its effects is evident in
the treatment ~ or rather
nontreatment ~ of the
scratched and worn
bedroom door, moldings,
and trim (above left), as
well as the window
moldings left unrestored
and bare (below left).
Crocheted bed coverlets
paired with heavy
khaki and cream-striped
canvas spreads and
a geometric-pattern rug
provide softness in
an otherwise austere
room (opposite).

GILDED SIMPLICITY

Only a very skillful mood-maker like Charles Spada could take two very different qualities ~ guilelessness and sophistication ~ and play them against each other so as to bring out the best in each. "I love incongruous things together," says the Boston-based interior designer. This Connecticut stone house, built a century ago by a Tuscan immigrant and refurbished by Spada, retains all the unpretentious roughness of an old-world dwelling. Yet its furnishings, mostly European antiques of good pedigree, reveal the cultivated tastes of an esthete.

In the renovation of the second-story bedroom, as in the rest of the once-disastrous interiors, Spada encouraged the rustic nature of the house, built from local stone and hand-mixed sand mortar, to shine through. The designer deliberately left the floors bare, bypassed wallpaper and printed fabrics, and used only white paint on walls restuccoed in the crude European manner.

The bedroom's original low pine ceilings (only 6 feet 8 inches high) and wide-board wood floors form an envelope for outstanding antiques. The highly polished woods of the eighteenth-century pieces and a gilded Italian mirror are lustrous against the matte finish of the stucco walls. The overall effect is intentionally spare. "When a room is terribly filled with color and objects," says Spada, "you can't concentrate on anything."

Deep-set casement windows reveal the sturdy construction of this old New England house. Shown off against the original wood ceiling and old wood floors of the master bedroom, fine antiques ~ a gilded Italian mirror, Swedish grain-painted writing table, cane-back French chair, and English bench set at the foot of the bed ~ add notes of sophistication and polish.

An early-nineteenth-century tea table of English oak and a headboard of inlaid Italian fruitwood are typical of the carefully chosen antiques that elevate the room above its simple architecture (above). A lush Italian painting of the late nineteenth century echoes the room's neutral palette (right). There are no bureaus or chests of drawers in this room; a new bank of closets and bookshelves, built in along one wall, fills all storage needs. The room's eclectic furnishings include a Syrian traveling chest inlaid with mother-of-pearl and ebonized and gilded Italian wall sconces (opposite).

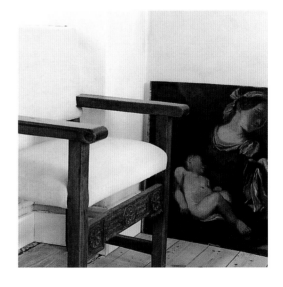

CHAPTER 2

Questions of Balance

The most successful decorating is often a delicate balancing act, a tightrope walk between playing it too safe and going over the top. A bedroom that is "all one thing" ~ religiously of a single style or period, say, or burdened with an overabundance of pattern, or spare without relief ~ can quickly become tiresome.

Dynamism comes from the conjunction of opposing elements, whether in terms of texture (the roughness of a sisal rug against the sheen of highly polished woods, for example), color (a jolt of bright red against a pale background), or attitude (a seashell on a fine antique piece).

Always, balance and harmony imply careful editing of furnishings and accessories. Sometimes, says designer De Bare Saunders, being out of scale is more interesting than being in scale. "Rules are for students," he says. For John Saladino, there is one abiding principle: "Things that go into a room must have respect for one another, even though those objects may be of totally opposite character. People who just jam everything into a beautiful room risk losing its proportions."

COOL AND CLASSIC

In the manner of his mentor, master decorator Billy Baldwin, Frank Babb Randolph often works with traditional elements ~ French furniture, fine antiques ~ and his approach often incorporates Baldwin principles such as using inexpensive fabrics on costly pieces of furniture. But the crisp lines of the bedrooms in his own home reveal the soul of a modernist.

Equilibrium in his Washington, D.C., bedroom begins with the bed itself: Centered in the room, it seems to float from the ceiling with the grace of a trapeze. The simple canopy, made from lengths of white cotton suspended from a thin wood frame, is open and airy, yet offers a sense of cozy enclosure. Although the room has 8-foot ceilings, "you feel you've entered a very grand room at least 10 feet tall," says Randolph.

The guest bedroom is as refined and carefully edited as the master bedroom ~ a kind of cool, clean extension of it, with snowy walls and tab curtains of the same burlap-textured linen. In both rooms, found objects such as shells picked up on the beach are mixed with expensive antique furnishings in yet another striking juxtaposition. "These are the things we see in nature," says the designer. "Why shouldn't we ive with them?"

In each room, furniture stands out in silhouette against the white walls and woodwork. A quiet backdrop, says Randolph, "makes furniture legs seem to dance."

In the master bedroom (opposite), light floods in through new clean-lined French doors hung with tab curtains of hand-woven Nantucket linen. A fine eighteenth-century chair wears natural-colored woven linen (above); designer Frank Babb Randolph's childhood teddy bear keeps things from becoming too serious.

The designer's democratic approach to decorating is evident in almost every corner, where fine antiques mingle with humbler pieces. In the guest room (above), where a large abstract painting sets the stage for a harmonious scheme of neutrals, an inexpensive wicker trunk for storing extra blankets hobnobs with a serious French antique chair.

Propped on the room's eighteenth-century Italian writing table is a gouache by American artist Willan de Looper (opposite).

ENGLISH COUNTRY UPDATED

E nglish country style" is often interpreted as a bower of floral prints. It's a look that can easily be overdone, even for aficionados. So when designer Mark Epstein was called upon to furnish a new Connecticut house using fabrics and upholstered pieces from Laura Ashley, a retailer whose name is practically synonymous with English country, his basic inclination toward simplicity provided welcome ballast for any potential floral excess.

With his associate William McGinn, Epstein created a bedroom that is comfortable and visually rich, yet free of superfluous detail. The expansive windows are partly sheathed in gauze instead of the more elaborate window treatment one might expect to find in such a room. Upholstery fabric was limited to just one floral pattern, and unpretentious sisal matting covers the floor.

The designer's adroit balancing act is evident in the contrast between the creamy monotone color scheme of the walls and floors, and liberal dashes of bright red in the bedskirt and on an upholstered ottoman. The open floor plan is loose and informal, a layout that also prevents the floral fabric from overwhelming the room. Casual country furniture ~ a stripped pine table used as a vanity, a Louis Philippe armoire typical of Provençal farmhouses ~ keeps the feeling light.

An expanse of small-paned windows, the room's outstanding architectural feature, was left mostly bare so as not to compete with the decor. A linen floral print was chosen for the English-style upholstered pieces. Texture is more important than pattern in the scheme of things: Rough sisal on the floor, a shiny red ottoman, and balloon shades of white gauze catch and hold the eye.

The notion of opposites playing off each other is evident even in this tabletop display (near right): A cleanly stripped pine table is used as an offbeat dressing table, with a glittery Venetian glass mirror, a neoclassical vase, and a bright red papier-mâché bowl. The French armoire behind it holds bed linens and books. An elegant hand-painted screen and silver breakfast service pair gracefully with a provincial antique "yo-yo" coverlet (below right). Against a buttery-cream background, the floral upholstery on an inviting loveseat and chair incorporates all the colors used throughout the room (far right).

POINT AND COUNTERPOINT

If an interior designer is like a symphony conductor, orchestrating harmonious agreement between disparate elements, then New York designer Mariette Himes Gomez is something of a maestro. Her trademark approach is a soothing envelope of pale color spiced with strong accents, including occasional doses of bright color, furnishings that make an architectural statement, and idiosyncratic accessories.

In her own Manhattan apartment, Gomez began with vanilla-colored walls, moldings, ceilings, and softly carpeted floor. This created a unifying backdrop for furnishings of different styles and periods, and had the additional advantage of making the apartment's two bedrooms each seem larger, as well as of a single harmonious piece. These two sophisticated rooms are so similar in their feeling of tranquility that they are almost extensions of one another.

Gomez disproves the old saw that small rooms must settle for scaled-down furniture. She chose large, important pieces, such as an eighteenth-century gilt and gesso Spanish headboard (gesso is a plasterlike substance used to prepare a surface for gilding or painting) and a circa 1850 Regency clothespress (essentially an armoire but with drawers at its base)

The sheltering sky of a landscape painting by contemporary artist Ben Schonzeit casts its tranquil vision over Mariette Himes Gomez' bedroom. Its lightness and calmness balance, in a quirky way, the imposing presence of the antique Spanish bed, with its ornate gilt and painted headboard.

for her own room, as well as a fanciful brass bedstead for her daughter's. And she manages to make it all work because there is little else besides the essentials in these two rooms. "Bedrooms are retreats," says Gomez. "I don't think closets and dressing tables should be part of places where one rests."

Touches of color ~ a piece of vintage chintz on an armchair in the designer's bedroom, a raspberry red chair and paisley throw at the foot of her daughter's elaborately curlicued brass bed ~ enliven the creamy palette here and there. Fine antique linens dress both beds, adding a special note of luxury and femininity. "I don't like anything too new," says the designer.

A perfect example of Gomez' sometimes quirky orchestration is the juxtaposition, in her bedroom, of a modern landscape painting above the elaborately carved bed. The painting is a worthy counterpart to the formidable bed in the strength of its imagery and in its equivalent width. The two pieces have no apparent thematic connection, but it is in their very difference that interest and harmony lie. "Together they create style," says Gomez. "It would be pretty boring to put a Madonna above that bed."

Billowing lace under-
curtains provide
a light counterpoint
to the master bedroom's
two massive pieces
of furniture: the bed and
an English Regency
clothespress, which stands
tall at its foot. The bed
wears a leaf-patterned
damask duvet cover;
the graceful chair is
upholstered in exuberant
vintage chintz.

Gomez furnished her
daughter's bedroom with
a nineteenth-century
embossed brass bed
bought in Peru (above
and right). A raspberry-
red-upholstered chair
and red wool paisley bed
throw boldly offset
the predominantly white
color scheme. Light
reflected off the mirror
at the foot of the bed
and through the diaph-
anous bed hangings
imparts a feminine,
ethereal quality.

Personal Taste

y their very private nature, bedrooms offer an opportunity to express personal style to its utmost. They are the perfect setting for a display of unabashed sentiment or idiosyncratic whimsy. All of us experience a sense of extra freedom and pleasure in decorating the bedroom. Less restricted by practicality than other rooms (the kitchen, certainly, or rooms where the television or computer dominates), we are obliged only to our own taste and comfort.

Comfort is key in the bedroom, and that comfort has a psychological dimension as well as a physical one. The bedroom is a place where our interior universe ~ the worlds of memory and fantasy ~ can come into play in subtle and mysterious ways. In the bedroom, favorite pictures, books, heirlooms, and items of sentimental significance contribute to comfort as much as do soft linens and pillows.

Thankfully, no one look dominates our era, as it did in times past. All the old "rules" have gone by the boards, and here, at the turn of the millennium, there is more room than ever in the bedroom for an individual point of view.

SCENE-STEALING STYLE

A muslin-tented bedroom with a polka-dot floor is not, perhaps, for everyone, but to Maine antiques dealer Corey Daniels, "theatrical" is synonymous with personal style. The room is one of fifteen in Daniels' eighteenth-century farmhouse, all furnished with pieces he had stashed away over the years, never knowing exactly where he would use them. Eventually they all found places in the house, whose decor may change radically from one season to the next.

He gave the freest rein to his creative impulses in this bedroom. "It started out as a joke, really," Daniels says of the exotic but inviting chamber, which recalls a Napoleonic-era campaign officer's tent. "It's more 'me' than any other room in the house." The quasi-military theme began as an effort to temper the raw, exposed beams of the peaked ceiling and to cover, quickly and cheaply,

unattractively painted wainscoting on the walls. Daniels' first proposed solution was to cut up an old canvas tent; failing that, he bought 100-yard rolls of muslin (for less than one dollar a yard) and began draping. The repeating border of heraldic trim that rings the room at the ceiling was cut from corrugated cardboard; it was born as a tongue-in-cheek allusion to tent flaps, as well as an attempt to cover the drapery tacks that held the muslin in place. As an impulsive final touch, Daniels decided to introduce pattern on the putty-colored wood floor by painting a loose design of white polka-dots.

A definitively masculine atmosphere prevails from the furniture to the accents: a brass campaign bed of the mid-nineteenth century, a heavy vintage trunk at its foot, the weighty terra-cotta jars from Crete, and an American pier table, all part of a subtle, muted palette of browns and golds.

A brass campaign bed, a sturdy spool-turned Victorian armchair, and an Anglo-Indian ebony chair emphasize the very masculine mood of Corey Daniels' tentlike bedroom. An American marble-topped pier table with columns serves as a miniature stage for an ever-changing array of objects, at present a vase with a painted profile and a serious-looking set of leather-bound books.

53

A pair of crossed spears and a costume jacket from a Shakespearean play hanging against the muslin drapery form a studied still life (left). The pieces make wry reference to theater and military campaigns, both of which inspired the room's decor. Gigantic terra-cotta jars occupy an unlikely perch near the ceiling.

In contrast with the meticulously staged master bedroom, the guest bedroom (opposite) has a more tranquil and generic ambience. Anybody can be comfortable in this nearly all-white room.

LAYERS OF MEANING

A bed angled rakishly in the bay window and taffeta curtains of pinkest pink are the first clues that here is a very non-conforming stylist indeed. Collage artist and textile designer Carolyn Quartermaine, who also owns a fabric and furnishings shop on London's fashionable Sloane Street, combines the avant-garde artist's sensibility with the traditionalist's predilection for pedigreed antique furnishings. "My style is a blend of the baroque and the contemporary," says Quartermaine. "I take things from the past and use fabrics and color to bring them up to date."

She approaches decorating the same way. "My environments have a sense of collage, of a buildup of paper, fabric, and furniture," she says. "I love hidden layers, revealed one at a time." In her delightfully glamorous London apartment-cum-workshop, part eighteenth-century French chateau and part present-day atelier, Quartermaine offers a decidedly contemporary take on the so-called feminine bedroom. Her own signature silks dress late-nineteenth-century Italian chairs; scribbled over with antique calligraphy, the fabrics take their inspiration from old French script and Mozart manuscripts. Eclectic flea-market finds and humble objects hobnob with formal antique furniture, which is angled casually against white walls with a modernist spareness that is clearly of this century.

Carolyn Quartermaine's roomful of unabashedly original flourishes includes the artist's hand-painted fabrics on a bench and gilded antique chairs, and a shock of brightest pink taffeta at the window. The nineteenth-century French bed "floats" away from the window into the center of the room.

Constantly changing
tableaux grace every
horizontal surface in
Quartermaine's
bedroom. On a marble
mantel (above left),
five carefully positioned
pinecones share space
with old glass vases
and a powder dish, as
well as with one of
Quartermaine's collages.

A lucite hat stand and
other personal treasures
make up a second
vignette (above right).
Mozart's manuscripts
inspired the artwork.
Stretched across a
bench is another of
Quartermaine's hand-
painted silks ~ this
one featuring cut-out
birdlike forms.

A *flotilla of late-nineteenth-century gilded Italian chairs wears Quartermaine's calligraphy-inspired silks. "I like the look of calligraphy, not what it says," the designer explains. "When I make collages out of calligraphy scraps, they take on a language of their own." The "door" between bedroom and bath is a simple, unadorned curtain; a peek into the romantic marble bathroom reveals a plaster copy of a Roman woman's head.*

CUTTING-EDGE CRAFTS

Stepping into the Manhattan apartment of Susie Elson, former chairwoman of the American Crafts Council and long-time crafts collector, is like entering a mad, mad world where the very idea of furniture has been wittily, sometimes bizarrely, reinvented. "It's far out of the ordinary," acknowledges Elson, who shares her high-ceilinged duplex with her husband, Edward Elliott Elson, the United States ambassador to Denmark. To achieve this pointedly individualistic decor, Elson commissioned all the furnishings from top artisans in their field.

Like a modern-day Medici, Elson is a patron of the art furniture world, giving craftspeople the freedom to create one-of-a-kind designs. "These are the antiques of the future," she believes. Things made years ago under her farsighted patronage still look very much of the moment. "If something is genuinely exciting," she says, "it will continue to be so." As if to prove the point, all the rooms in the sunlit apartment are filled with wonderful handcrafted oddities ~ including a cubist-inspired grand piano with exaggerated geometric planes and trapezoidal legs and twisted-metal chairs in the shape of human figures. "I like things that have a sense of humor, that are on the cutting edge," she says.

In the master bedroom, the dominating presence is a contemporary interpretation of a historic four-poster bed, the posts punched through with Swiss-cheese-like holes. The guest bedroom, in turn, features a writing table and chair from an avant-garde Japanese workshop; its adjoining sitting room nods to craftsmen of the past with a showcase filled with Greek and Roman antiquities. "A bedroom is a place where one spends a great deal of time," says Elson. "It should have joie de vivre, not be staid or humdrum."

In the guest bedroom, a freewheeling mix of animal-print fabrics dresses the bed. In one corner a Japanese writing table holds a collection of ceramic bowls and framed prints; the chair, also Japanese, is distinguished by a metal sunburst back and a seat of lacquered wood. The sitting room beyond is furnished with a classic piece by Le Corbusier and a postmodern tower cabinet from Germany.

For the master bedroom
(right), Edward Zucca
made a four-poster
bed of bleached maple,
then finished it with silver
leaf and black ebony
detailing. A glass-top
table by Peter Pierborn
has seven unmatching
ebony legs (above).
The aluminum wing-back
angel chair, by Mark
Brazier-Jones, features
a plump upholstered
velvet seat sitting atop
legs with eyeballs.

CHAPTER 4

Surface Appearances

I t all begins with the envelope ~ floors, ceilings, walls, and even windows. The surfaces that enclose a bedroom ~ whether a snug guest hideaway tucked under a sloping roof or a sleek and spacious master suite ~ define its proportions and give the space its basic character. From these fundamental relationships a design can evolve. Sometimes one compelling physical attribute can be the starting point for the design that follows. Perhaps the ceilings are rustic wood beams of an old country church, or the walls are made of translucent glass block, or there is an expanse of beautifully aged wood floors.

Often the dictates of location or even climate are so important that choices of materials are narrowed down. Tile makes more sense than carpet in an Arizona bedroom, for example, while windows with a magnificent view require a different approach from those that face a busy street.

Even if the starting point is an unadorned room with walls of simple sheetrock and floors of plain wood, it is an invitation to the designer to address the envelope ~ and perhaps even push it a bit.

To sound an upbeat
note in this spacious bedroom, designer Gary
Paul chose an unusual,
hand-painted wallpaper
~ a lighthearted takeoff
on a conventional
buttoned-down stripe.
The curtain panels
are made of raw silk. A
new Chinese needlepoint
rug in the Aubusson style
was chosen for the way
its beige ground and mint
green and pink detail tie
in with the wallpaper's
coloring, and for the way
its formal pattern plays
against the verticality of
the painterly walls.

A tiny bedroom tucked under a steep-pitched roof in this Colorado house features rough plaster and old wooden beams salvaged from a tumbledown building nearby. The room's enormous character belies the fact that this is a newly built retreat. Lacy bed-clothes provide an unexpected counterpoint to all the rusticity.

The restored flower beds outside ~ originally planted by Louise Beebe Wilder, a famous garden writer of the early 1900s ~ inspired the decor of this country bedroom in upstate New York. Designer David Easton installed new French doors so that the room would "reach out to nature." Oak ceiling beams stained to look old remind the owner of summers spent in France. The French terra-cotta tile floor "flows" in from adjoining rooms.

"Bringing the outside in" was a tenet of mid-century modernism; this house, designed by Bauhaus architect Marcel Breuer in the 1950s, is almost an extension of the natural landscape. In one bedroom (opposite), walls of rugged Maryland stone, carefully placed to show off its shape and color, create a powerful abstract composition. The huge glass sliding doors extend the space visually into the woods. In another bedroom (above), a bluestone floor is a cool complement to the woven grasscloth "wainscoting" and nubby wall hangings. The wall-hung desk and credenza echo the low horizontal lines of the house.

CONCRETE REFLECTIONS

Sunlight, and its reflection on water, are prime elements in the decoration of this contemporary Florida home. All the main rooms in the vast, E-shaped house are organized around a 47-foot swimming pool that comes almost to the ground-level windows. Light bounces off the swimming pool through the square-mullioned, floor-to-ceiling windows, penetrating the house even in winter when the sun is at a low angle. It flickers on white walls and floors made of summerstone, a precast concrete paving material that runs through the house and outside into the pool courtyard. "Water is a great architectural tool," says Washington, D.C., architect Hugh Newell Jacobsen. "It was an intentional part of the design."

In a highly practical choice of materials, the designer paved the master bedroom with the same summerstone, a textured snow-white material that has imprints of coral in it. He continued the summerstone right through the bedroom's sybaritic bath, a freestanding little pavilion linked to the bedroom by a corridor. Nonslippery and treated with waterproof sealant, this flooring is ideal for a house where trekking between the pool and the interior goes on all day. It also helps keep the rooms cool. To minimize the need for air-conditioning, every room was designed with two exposures for cross-ventilation and relies on ceiling fans to keep the air moving.

But the main feature of the house remains the light and its reflections. The bedroom walls and ceilings wear a straightforward coat of flat white paint, forming a clean, contemporary canvas on which light and its interplay on water act out their dramatic roles.

Architect Hugh Newell Jacobsen's passion for classical order and symmetry is expressed in the windows in the master bedroom, which run the full 10 feet from floor to ceiling. Jacobsen also designed the four-poster bed, made of steel pipe with faux bronze finish, specifically for the room.

The bath pavilion, with an oval tub sunk into white summerstone flooring, features a ceiling-high door to the garden beyond (left). A grove of grapefruit trees shields the room from view, but tall louvered shutters can be closed for greater privacy.

The adjoining master bedroom (opposite), a classic white box with unadorned plasterboard walls and ceiling and the same summerstone flooring, might seem antiseptic in cooler climes; in subtropical Florida, its coolness is welcome.

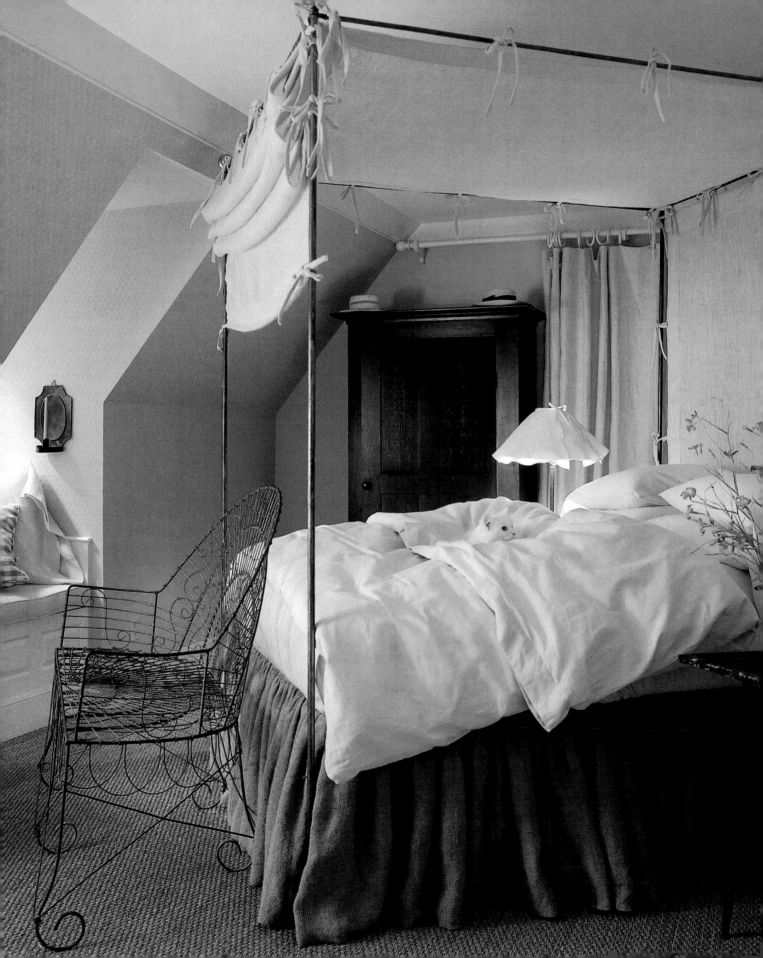

CHAPTER 5

Beds and Beyond

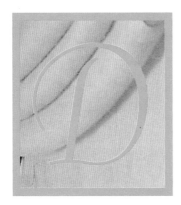

aybed, sleigh bed, or canopy bed ~ a bed is, of course, the one given in a bedroom, and by virtue of its significance as much as its size, it generally occupies center stage. But even given its preeminence, a bed may be imposing or retiring, formal or informal. The traditional four-poster, for example, will immediately assert its sturdy presence in the largest room. But the curtains and lines of the contemporary four-poster can impart a lightness unknown to its medieval forebears.

A simple bed, such as a futon on a platform, will allow other pieces to establish the mood of the room ~ an antique armoire, perhaps, or an inviting armchair. Auxiliary pieces ~ desk, chairs, vanity, nightstand ~ should do more than look pretty. "Everything must be functional," says designer De Bare Saunders. "Even an antique desk should have a useful writing surface, not just be there for decoration."

Freed from the "matched suites" that once enjoyed great popularity, we can forage through history for inspiration. It is only fitting that in this most personal room, furniture is mixed and matched ~ old with new, antiques with reproductions ~ to personalize the space.

Manhattan designer Debra Blair chose reproduction furniture with an exotic Anglo-Indian look ~ a metal bed with a tent-shaped top, left bare except for sheer batiste drapery panels, and a cane and teak "planter's chaise" ~ for a show-house bedroom. Indian rugs over textured sisal on the floor, glazed pomegranate-red walls, and a cerulean-blue ceiling form a rich tableau.

Quirky and colorful, with red and white floral-papered walls and turquoise floors, this bedroom by Brian Murphy of the venerable Parish-Hadley decorating firm is anchored by a four-poster bed with pineapple finials. An African-American snake quilt (intended to keep evil spirits away while its owner sleeps) and a 1950s circular hooked rug with a sea-creature motif add even more layers of pattern.

The elegant curvature
of the iron four-poster
bed echoes this bedroom's
distinctive tentlike ceiling.
Atlanta designer Nancy
Braithwaite chose
reproduction pieces for
this house ~ Regency-style
carved gilt armchairs
and a French Empire-
style cherry center table ~
as counterpoints to the
room's contemporary
architecture. Sunny yellow-
striped walls, sumptuous
bed hangings, and white
silk upholstery on the
sofa convey cheerfulness
and elegance in equal
measure. A yellow and
white linen print borders
the white damask bed
hangings, pillows, and
bedskirt, as well as the
Roman shades.

This inviting nap spot and sometime guest room occupies one end of a long narrow kitchen in the Kansas City house of decorative arts dealers Bruce Burstert and Robert Raymond Smith. They sought out indigenous American furniture ~ a Missouri-made walnut daybed more than 150 years old, a slip-covered chaise, an American Queen Anne-style tea table, and a New England cupboard still wearing its original red paint ~ to complement the house's colonial design roots.

Pride of place in this cozy bedroom under the eaves of a Martha's Vineyard seaside estate goes to a custom-made copy of a traditional Empire sleigh bed. The commodious curves of its headboard and footboard make it a compelling focal point in the small room.

For decoration, New York design team Tom Fox and Joe Nahem capitalized on the owners' collection of antique fishing lures. A vintage electric fan hums with a nostalgic whirr.

A quick and clever solution to the question of privacy in a guest room shared by twin beds is this freestanding, three-part screen. Painted to look like button-tufted upholstery, the screen separates the beds, at the same time effectively carving out a nook for a dressing table. Simple wood bedsteads and a color scheme of pale blues and creams create the feeling of a classic Swedish country interior.

Designer Glenn Gissler turned a cozy seaside bedroom into a sitting room with an upholstered twin-size bed (above). A custom-built oak frame and piles of pillows further disguise the bed. An Asian storage box cov- ered with parchment serves as a coffee table.

A charmingly sedate guest bedroom in a rural New Jersey farmhouse is furnished with a French Empire enameled metal sleigh bed and an antique English sewing table used as a night- stand (opposite). The idea, says Jorge Letelier, the architect who owns this weekend home, was to evoke the feeling of a fine old country house in Brittany.

Headwords can be a functional backrest and a decorative focal point of almost architectural importance. Here, Mariette Himes Gomez joined twin-size mahogany Empire headboards with bronze d'oré trim to make a king-size bed. A tall nineteenth-century screen behind the headboard gives the bed still greater height.

A *lacy scrollwork head-board* is the outstanding decorative feature in a bedroom where under-statement rules. Like a pen and ink drawing on a blank page, its silhouette is sharp against the room's subtle patterns and textures. On the bed, for example, though everything is white, the matte linen duvet, shams, and bedskirt contrast with the sheen of the pillowcases and top sheet. A *classical medallion* and swag cotton print on an antique chair at the foot of the bed is another decorative flourish.

A fabulous Art Nouveau bentwood bed by the Thonet Brothers furniture makers, found in a Paris flea market, is part of a wide-ranging selection of decorative arts in a Connecticut collector's home (above). The curvaceous loveseat is also a nineteenth-century European bentwood piece. White walls and simple bed dressings allow the strong, sinuous lines to dominate the room.

A distinguished guest bedroom in Jorge Letelier's New Jersey country house features an antique metal bed from Italy, an Empire chair, and a Greek revival urn lamp on a skirted table (opposite). In such refined surroundings, the choice of art on the wall ~ a contemporary painting of suburban houses and mailboxes in lurid colors ~ comes as a bit of a shock. "I find it fresh, friendly, and amusing," says the designer ~ a reminder "not to take things so seriously."

Trim yet glamorous, this bedroom by Los Angeles designer Michael Berman relies on large-scale pieces for impact (left). A sheet-metal sleigh bed with Art Deco curves combines with an imposing fruit-wood armoire (housing an audio-video system), a spirited pair of roll-arm club chairs in bold black and cream stripe, and an oval ottoman with long cord trimming. Celadon green walls form a soothing backdrop. The designer's X-legged writing table and wool-upholstered chair (above), with its voluptuous form and satin-finish legs, take inspiration from such 1940s masters as Jean-Michel Frank and T. H. Robsjohn-Gibbings.

*Genuine antiques mix
unabashedly with
reproductions against the
wood-paneled wall
of a nineteenth-century
farmhouse bedroom
in upstate New York. The
low poster bed ~ simple,
graceful, and strong of
line ~ is newly made, as
are the slipcovered
club chairs and ottoman.
The circular end table
in the foreground
is a contemporary craft
piece. Everything else ~
the faded Oriental rug,
weighty silver candlestick,
vintage velvet throw
pillows, and toile de Jouy
bed covering ~ has
been mellowed and soft-
ened by time.*

There's nothing more gracious or convenient than a separate room reserved for getting dressed. Mariette Himes Gomez took the space seriously, choosing furniture of consequence, including a gleaming Empire dresser and an English chaise longue with a hinged cushion that opens for storage (opposite). Clear panes of glass in all the doors were replaced with mirrors. Beige basket-weave carpeting sets the room apart from the adjoining master bedroom, which has bare floors.

Storage pieces need not always be used in the room for which they were intended. In the Newport, Rhode Island, summer house bedroom of the late interior designer Robert Hill, an antique French kitchen hutch has been pressed into service as a bookcase (above). Its distressed white finish helps the piece blend easily with the white-stained oak floors and soft gray-beige walls that form the pale envelope of the room.

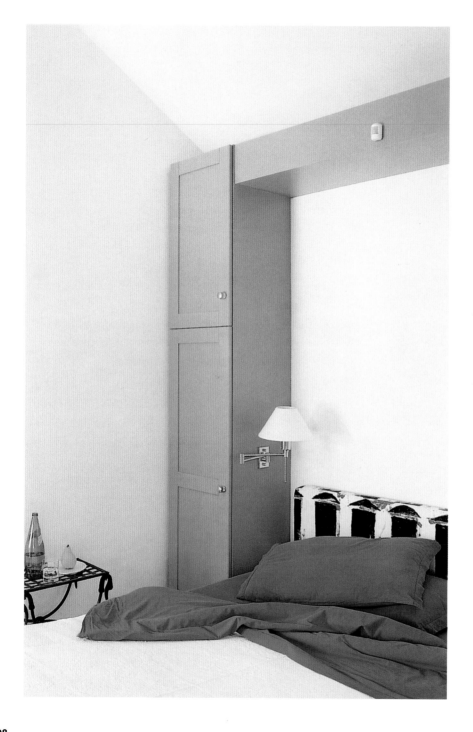

These compact storage
cupboards were designed
by Milan-based architect
Gae Aulenti for a friend's
seaside retreat (left).
In keeping with a week-
end house whose focus
is the outdoors, most of
the furniture is kept
simple and is built-in.

A freestanding storage
unit (opposite) is the
centerpiece of a commodi-
ous dressing room in
a new suburban house
by architects Shelton,
Mindel. Resembling
a giant jewelry box, it
opens on all four sides,
revealing a dressing
table within.

*Atlanta decorator
Jane Williamson devised
a charming, feminine
vanity to just fit in front
of a sunny window
(opposite). The serpentine
front was cut from
plywood, then smocked
like a little girl's dress
with red and white
ribbon-patterned fabric.*

*Long Island designer
Pat Sayers chose historic
lilac-pattern fabric,
topped with a piece of lace
cutwork, to form the
dressing table skirt (right).
Beneath the surface is
a simple, white-painted
plywood box with cubby
holes for storage.*

SOLID COMFORTS

T here is not a piece of furniture in this urbane bedroom designed for a gentleman that does not have serious presence. Each carefully chosen item stands by itself; some, like a Biedermeier bed and turn-of-the-century Austrian desk, are practically small buildings in their own right.

All of this is, of course, no accident. "The room itself was modern and somewhat lackluster," says designer De Bare Saunders, "so we chose furniture of great architectural interest." The pieces were selected individually, not all purchased at one time. "We put little in, but each piece is in scale with the others and with the architecture of the room," says Saunders. The pediment-topped headboard on that remarkable bed, for example, reminds the designer and his partner, Ronald Mayne, of the Italian Renaissance architect Palladio (in the oval is an exquisite oil painting of Mercury tying his shoe). The substantial armchair is a leather reproduction of a classic Art Deco design. Amid all this solidness of form, the charcoal and ivory zebra-striped rug makes a bold graphic statement of its own, as does the striped wallpaper, whose camel color complements the wood tones of the furniture.

What makes it all work? "Everything's very clean-lined, no matter what period or century," says Saunders. "It was all modern for its day."

There are no "throw-away" pieces in this masculine bedroom created by Ronald Mayne and De Bare Saunders. Everything from the austerely simple Austrian desk to the leather arm-chair stands on solid, almost sculptural ground.

An 1890s gilded
vanity mirror, set within
a Corinthian temple
frame, echoes the
pedimented headboard it
reflects (left). Its richness
is balanced by a tailored
striped chintz on the gentleman's dressing table
and tempered by personal
mementos tucked into
the frame of the mirror.
Painted gold flowers
adorn the backrest of a
Chinese black lacquer
chair. The streamlined
leather armchair offers
an irresistible place
to read (opposite). At the
window, a valance and
cafe curtain of seersucker
trimmed with unfussy
cotton fringe and hung
loosely from curtain
tiebacks allow a soft light
to penetrate the room.

CHAPTER 6

Dressing the Room

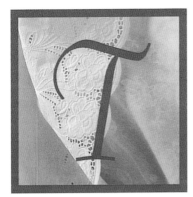

The lavish use of fabric in a bedroom still signifies what it did in Louis XIV's France: luxury. The swags, festoons, and tassels of brocade, damask, and silk in a fashionable seventeenth-century boudoir also provided privacy and a certain degree of warmth against the elements. But by the late nineteenth century, interest in the healthful effects of fresh air led to a much lighter, fresher look. Today, anything goes.

Today's fabrics of choice may be gauzy white cottons, ever-popular chintzes (whose lush floral patterns are still based on nineteenth-century favorites), natty stripes, carefree checks, or restful solids, which can be an antidote to the profusion of pattern often found elsewhere in the house.

Fabric-covered furniture ~ headboard, chairs, skirted vanity ~ provide additional opportunities to experiment. Pretty pleats and even contrasting piping can unify several different pieces and lend a layer of eye-catching detail. In recent years, sheets ~ prehemmed, seamless, and in marvelous patterns ~ have made department stores a wonderful resource for decorating the bedroom.

This voluminously draped pine four-poster belonging to designer and writer Alexandra Stoddard is a cocoon from which its occupants can enjoy a fire in the facing hearth. The white hangings fall in a generous floor-length flounce, tamed by the crispness of blue and white striped pillows and a classic American quilt (above).

Pillowcases and sheets patterned with overscaled roses and an heirloom quilt in a classic star pattern make this attic bedroom look soulful and sweet (opposite).

Oceans of fabric in the colors of sunshine and ripe fruit ~ mainly a printed French cotton combining floral and paisley motifs ~ elevate this grandly proportioned showhouse bedroom to levels of fantasy reminiscent of England's Royal Pavilion in Brighton. The custom canopy, made of thick swags of fabric cascading from a conical crown known as a lit à la Polonaise, and a V-shaped window valance trimmed with tinkly gold bells are delightfully fanciful. "I didn't want anything stodgy or uptight," says designer Barbara Ostrom. Upholstered panels on the headboard and footboard match the fabric on the bolster and bedcover, to add an aura of coziness.

In a room that is a model of Zen understatement, with a controlled palette of sandy neutrals, carefully tailored bed-linens take center stage (above). The soft-toned duvet cover and pillowcases on the low platform bed give the room a contemporary, tailored look. Striped edging and buttons on the pillows are handsome details (left).

Demure, fresh fabrics ~ lacy Victorian whites on the bed, a striped ticking slipcover on a chaise ~ stir memories of childhood summers in the master bedroom of a new Ozark retreat (opposite). The nostalgic atmosphere warms up a sparsely furnished room, whose few pieces are contributions from the owners' relatives and friends.

There is no shortage of
fabric in this serene
creation by Boston
designer Benn Theodore
(opposite). A cushioned
upholstered headboard in
cream cotton harmonizes
with the clipped Swiss
batiste bed hangings that
dress the four-poster.
European linens cover a
profusion of pillows.

A matching bench curls
up at the foot of the bed.
    A Connecticut
antiques dealer who
loves the plain lines of
Shaker furniture
created these tidy-as-a-
bandbox bed enclosures
(above). Fresh and
crisp, the draped alcoves
provide drama in a
Shaker-plain guest room.

The headboards, bed-
skirts, and canopy
linings of blue plaid
are in simple but
striking contrast to the
expanses of white.

For the master bedroom
of his eighteenth-century
house, the late designer
and trompe l'oeil artist
Richard Lowell Neas had
the bedspread, head-
board, and ornamental
canopy hand-quilted in a
local village. The bed's
scalloped baldequin-
shaped headboard has
a look of provincial
formality. The wall's
molding and paneling
are actually paint on
plaster walls.

This deceptively casual showhouse bedroom by French designer Yves Taralon ~ a sea of taupe sparked with crisp white linens ~ perfectly illustrates how fabric can be used in a handsome, masculine way. The room's masterstroke: walls draped with sumptuous woven damask that can be easily changed or pushed aside to reach concealed closets; the fabric also provides good insulation against drafts. The bed's simple canopy is of the soft, supple wool flannel more commonly used for men's suiting. Black and white striped grosgrain trim on the headboard and a tailored bedskirt add a heraldic touch.

In this cool, orderly bedroom, Boston designer Richard Eustice used just two fabrics ~ a classic linen stripe in cream and brown for bed, windows, windowseat, and pillows and a white cotton duck, quilted in a diamond pattern, for nonrumpling slipcovers. The striped fabric was cut into squares and reassembled to make a patchwork bedspread (right). The window shades feature pleated lambrequins.

Fabric gives the interior of this Derbyshire gatehouse in England its cheerful demeanor. Sunny yellow enlivens the polka-dot walls and the exuberant floral chintz curtains. A delicate red and white stripe covers the whimsically shaped headboard, while broader and bolder versions of the stripe appear on the bedspread and pillow.

In a small London bedroom, decorator Lady Jane Churchill took a cue from France, where bedrooms are often decorated with just one patterned fabric. Here a charming red and white toile de Jouy upholsters the walls and headboard and swaths the windows. A rosy red braided trim is used to highlight curtain details and give the scheme greater definition. White lace-trimmed linens and pillows make the bed an oasis of calm.

TAILOR-MADE TRANQUILITY

Soothing is the word for this bedroom by designers Charles Spada and Tom Vanderbeck. The color gray, which is often underrated and surprisingly versatile, is the key to this pleasant effect. "I love gray in bedrooms because it's soft, ethereal, and calming," says Spada.

To make the room look all of a piece despite its collection of antique furnishings from disparate sources, the designers used a palette of grays and limited the number of fabrics to just a few unfussy ones. "Forget about heavy lace, chintzes, and brocades," says Spada. "Keep a bedroom minimal, so it's not overbearing. In a bedroom you want to feel calm, not be distracted by a mishmash of things."

For the curtains, tailored bedskirt, headboard, and chaise longue, Spada and Vanderbeck chose a cotton-linen blend, a material they find more practical than linen, which tends to rumple. The custom-made draperies feature inverted pleats, rather than the more traditional pinch pleats, to achieve a richer, fuller, more refined look. A pair of late-nineteenth-century painted French chairs are covered in linen; a little gold footstool is upholstered in gray silk taffeta. Touches of white ~ a strip of edging along the bottom of the bedskirt, simple bed linens ~ provide a refreshing contrast.

Not a ruche or a ruffle finds its way into this smart, tailored bedroom. The headboard is upholstered in a soft gray cotton-linen blend; the bedskirt is of the same fabric edged in white. "Bedrooms shouldn't be overfrilly and suffocating," believes designer Charles Spada. "You can come into this room, take a deep breath, and forget the world."

Consistency of color in fabric and paint unifies an assortment of antique European pieces (left). An eighteenth-century French chaise, still bearing its original paint, and the headboard (above) have been upholstered in a durable cotton-linen blend. The demilune commode has a coat of distressed paint that matches the gray fabric.

Final Touches

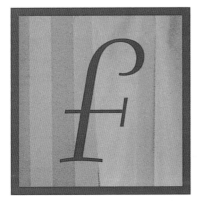

or many of us when it comes to accessorizing a bedroom, minimalism is not a very appealing concept. Sentimental souvennirs should find a natural home here ~ a pair of antique candlesticks, a vintage radio, some seashells from a vacation, beloved family photographs, favorite books. Together they contribute to the sense of well-being that is the essence of every successful bedroom.

Unlike large pieces of furniture, accents ~ small collectibles, pillows, artwork, for example ~ are easy to vary. Since we spend a lot of time in the bedroom it is important to head off visual ennui. One antiques dealer suggests removing all small objects from time to time and creating new vignettes by bringing pieces out of storage or borrowing them from other rooms. Careful placement and well-conceived displays can make even the most ordinary accessories seem special. "Every object needs a home," says New York designer Mariette Himes Gomez. "When your possessions don't have a home in your bedroom, they're simply clutter. When they're well organized, they become collections."

The repetition of a single simple shape produces a striking wall display in this bedroom by decorator Jeff Lincoln. With little else to distract the eye, the two tiers of six framed antique engravings, viewed through the lines of an undraped iron four-poster, create a harmonious geometry. A pair of white plaster table lamps on either side of the bed, reproductions of a classic Giacometti disc design of the 1940s, underscores the room's decisive symmetry. A carved wooden pineapple, once a finial on the roof of an old building, was chosen for its sculptural quality and hefty scale.

Sparkling accessories play off an intense backdrop of sage-green walls in a crisply elegant bedroom by designers Lee Bierly and Christopher Drake (left). Against this color a gilt-framed bull's-eye mirror stands out. Beneath, an antique mirrored chest is home to a framed drawing on an easel and a pair of candlestick lamps.

Glints of gold and hints of grandeur reminiscent of the Old South are artfully combined in a Louisiana bedroom by designers Ann Holden and Ann Dupuy (opposite). The gold beaded lampshade and gilt sunburst mirror frames add iridescent detail. The cherub hanging from the wrought-iron bed frame adds an unexpected note of whimsy.

A purist ethic, very much in keeping with the traditional Japanese approach to choosing and positioning objects, is at work in this Manhattan high-rise bedroom belonging to design consultant Robert Homma. A century-old statue of Buddha sits atop a lacquered table (opposite). The screen, a contemporary piece made of handmade paper, was picked up at a department store sale. A trio of boldly patterned shells creates a strong still life on a patterned bench. Green vases by a Japanese ceramicist are arrayed on a nineteenth-century scholar's bench traditionally used for calligraphy (above). A contemporary red and gold Japanese lacquer box is used for photo storage, while Shunga prints and woodcuts are propped casually against the wall.

Even books become decorative accessories when displayed in a glass-fronted Empire bookcase with old-world charm (opposite). The all-white pottery on the cabinet is one of several collections grouped by color in the Victorian farmhouse of designer Jorge Letelier.

An ever-changing array of objects and art-work marks the decorating style of antiques dealer Corey Daniels (right). This studied bedside arrangement is composed of vintage treasures: twin mercury glass vases, old framed photographs, and an alabaster decanter.

HOMESPUN TRADITION

A love for all things old and handcrafted informs the decor of two bedrooms in the studio of Bob Timberlake, a painter of the American Realist school who also is something of a cultural historian. Timberlake oversees the production of a line of furniture and accessories that captures and preserves the Arts and Crafts heritage of North Carolina, his home state.

To complement native folk furnishings found in the area ~ pie safes with hand-punched tin panels, painted chests, and twig rockers, for example ~ Timberlake collects and reproduces homespun accessories. Among them are quilts, coverlets, pottery (including agateware pitchers), birdhouses, and decoys. All are locally made in the manner of master craftspeople of the past. Pottery bowls are hand thrown and decorated with simple red, blue, and brown glazes typical of the region. Rag rugs are woven on looms just as they were a century ago. Wooden furniture such as beds and chairs are finished to show off the distinctive grains of native cherry and walnut.

Above all, Timberlake appreciates "the way things were made with such love and affection back in the old days," with an innate love of materials ~ the woods, the homespun, the clay ~ that were transformed into furniture, quilts, and pots to be cherished.

The rough-hewn beams and small window of a restored 1807 log home form an authentic setting for reproduction furnishings and accessories with roots in rural North Carolina crafts traditions. In the master bedroom, a chest is hand-painted with Pennsylvania Dutch motifs, and a new quilt reproduces the vivid log cabin pattern. A collection of beautifully framed silhouettes punctuates the geometry of the log-chinking walls.

Vintage toys recalling
a country childhood ~
birchbark canoes on
the wall, a red metal truck
on a sidetable ~ acces-
sorize a guest bedroom in
Bob Timberlake's studio.
A wall shelf above the easy
chair holds a handful
of miniatures. A rag rug,
camp blankets, and boldly
striped bed covers bring
high color to the rustic
decor. Worn blue paint on
a reproduction cabinet
convincingly simulates age.

Directory of Designers and Architects

Gae Aulenti
Dott.Arch.Gae.Aulenti
Milan, Italy

Michael Berman
Michael Berman Design
Los Angeles, California

Lee Bierly
Bierly-Drake
Boston, Massachusetts

Debra Blair
Blair Design Associates, Inc.
New York, New York

Nancy Braithwaite
Nancy Braithwaite Interiors, Inc.
Atlanta, Georgia

Bruce Burstert
Robert Raymond Smith Oriental
    Rugs and Bruce Burstert
    Decorative Arts
Kansas City, Missouri

Manuel Canovas
Manuel Canovas, Inc.
New York, New York

Paul Canvasser
PDC Designer
Birmingham, Michigan

Jane Churchill
Jane Churchill Interiors Ltd.
London, England

Celeste Cooper
Repertoire
Boston, Massachusetts

Corey Daniels
Corey Daniels Antiques
Wells, Maine

Christopher Drake
Bierly-Drake
Boston, Massachusetts

Ann Dupuy
Holden & Dupuy
New Orleans, Louisiana

David Easton
David Anthony Easton, Inc.
New York, New York

Mark Epstein
Mark Epstein Associates
New York, New York

Richard Eustice
Atlantic House Ltd.
Boston, Massachusetts

Tom Fox
Fox-Nahem Design
New York, New York

Lynn Gerhard
Gerhard Designs
Islip, New York

Glenn Gissler
Glenn Gissler Design, Inc.
New York, New York

Mariette Himes Gomez
Gomez Associates
New York, New York

Carolyn Guttilla
Carolyn Guttilla / Plaza One
Locust Valley, New York

Albert Hadley
Parish-Hadley Associates
New York, New York

Ann Holden
Holden & Dupuy
New Orleans, Louisiana

Cathi and Steven House
House + House
San Francisco, California

Hugh Newell Jacobsen
Hugh Newell Jacobsen
Washington, D.C.

Jorge Letelier
Letelier-Rock Design, Inc.
New York, New York

Jeffrey T. Lincoln
Jeffrey Lincoln Interiors Inc.
Locust Valley, New York

Ronald Mayne
Stingray Hornsby Antiques
 and Interiors
Watertown, Connecticut

Lee Mindel
Shelton, Mindel and Associates
New York, New York

Brian Murphy
Parish-Hadley Associates, Inc.
New York, New York

Joe Nahem
Fox-Nahem Design
New York, New York

Barbara Ostrom
Barbara Ostrom Associates, Inc.
Mahwah, New Jersey

Gary Paul
Gary Paul Design, Inc.
New York, New York

Peter Pennoyer
Peter Pennoyer Architects PC
New York, New York

Carolyn Quartermaine
London, England

Frank Babb Randolph
Frank Babb Randolph Interior
 Design
Washington, D.C.

Craig Raywood
Craig Raywood Design, 401 Ltd.
New York, New York

Katie Ridder
Peter Pennoyer Architects PC
New York, New York

Spruce Roden
VSF
New York, New York

John Saladino
John F. Saladino, Inc.
New York, New York

De Bare Saunders
Stingray Hornsby Antiques
 and Interiors
Watertown, Connecticut

Pat Sayers
Design Resources of Long
 Island Inc.
Huntington, New York

Peter Shelton
Shelton, Mindel and Associates
New York, New York

Robert Raymond Smith
Robert Raymond Smith Oriental
 Rugs and Bruce Burstert
 Decorative Arts
Kansas City, Missouri

Charles Spada
Charles Spada Interiors
Boston, Massachusetts

Alexandra Stoddard
Alexandra Stoddard, Inc.
New York, New York

Yves Taralon
Yves-Germain Taralon
 Decoration
Richebourg, France

Benn Theodore
Benn Theodore, Inc.
Boston, Massachusetts

Tom Vanderbeck
T. F. Vanderbeck Antiques
 and Interiors
Hadlyme, Connecticut

Peter Wheeler
P. J. Wheeler Associates
Boston, Massachusetts

Jane Williamson
Jane Williamson Antiques
 and Design
Atlanta, Georgia

The room on page 1 was designed by Jane Churchill; page 2, Vincent Dané; page 7, Barbara Deichman; page 8, Bruce Burstert and Robert Raymond Smith; page 11, Ann Holden and Ann Dupuy; page 16, Lynn Gerhard; page 34, Celeste Cooper; page 50, Craig Raywood; page 64, Cathi and Steven House; page 76, Nancy Braithwaite; page 126, Charles Spada; page 142, Robert Hill.

Photography Credits

1	Christopher Simon Sykes	66	James Yochum	109	Kari Haavisto	
2	Michael Dunne	67	Laurie E. Dickson	110-111	Jeff McNamara	
4	Kari Haavisto	68-69	John Vaughan	112	Esto/Scott Frances (top and bottom)	
7	J. Merrell	70-71	Walter Smalling	113	Richard Felber	
8	Peter Margonelli	72	Robert Lautman	114	Eric Roth	
11	Lizzie Himmel	74-75	Robert Lautman	115	David Phelps	
12	Kari Haavisto	76	Jack Winston	116	Jacques Dirand	
15	Scott Frances	78	Jeff McNamara	117	Walter Smalling	
16	Jeff McNamara	79	Jeff McNamara	118-119	Jeff McNamara	
18	Richard Felber	80-81	Langdon Clay	120	Simon Wheeler	
20-21	Richard Felber	82	Peter Margonelli	121	Christopher Simon Sykes	
22	Antoine Bootz	83	Lizzie Himmel	122	Jeff McNamara	
24-25	Antoine Bootz	84-85	Scott Frances	124-125	Jeff McNamara	
26	Lizzie Himmel	86	Andrew Bordwin	126	Antoine Bootz	
28-29	Lizzie Himmel	87	Jeff McNamara	128-129	Peter Margonelli	
30	Antoine Bootz	88	Antoine Bootz	130	Eric Roth	
32-33	Antoine Bootz	89	William Waldron	131	Lizzie Himmel	
34	Tom Yee	90	Catherine Leuthold	132-133	Antoine Bootz	
36-39	Gordon Beall	91	Jeff McNamara	134	Jeff McNamara	
40	Antoine Bootz	92-93	Grey Crawford	135	Thibault Jeanson	
42-43	Antoine Bootz	94-95	Kari Haavisto	136	Langdon Clay	
44	Thibault Jeanson	96	Antoine Bootz	138-139	Langdon Clay	
46-49	Thibault Jeanson	97	Thibault Jeanson	10	Thibault Jeanson	
50	Antoine Bootz	98	Antoine Bootz			
52	Thibault Jeanson	99	Langdon Clay			
54-55	Thibault Jeanson	100	Walter Smalling			
56	Jacques Dirand	101	Jeff McNamara			
58-60	Jacques Dirand	102	Kit Latham			
62-63	Jacques Dirand	104-105	Kit Latham			
64	Christopher Irion	106	Kari Haavisto			
		108	Elizabeth Zeschin			

Index

Acknowledgments

House Beautiful would like to thank the following homeowners: Jeffrey and Sharon Casdin, Lynn and Kurt Kircher, Pat Guthman, David and Katrin Cargill, Dolph Leuthold, Suzanne and Elliott West.

The photograph on page 16 was taken at the Mansions and Millionaires Showhouse, Sands Point, New York; page 34, the Boston Design Center, Boston, Massachusetts; page 66, the Park Ridge Youth Campus Showhouse, Wilmette, Illinois; page 78, the Mansions in May Showhouse, Morristown, New Jersey; pages 79 and 86, the Southampton Showhouse, Southampton, New York; page 88, the Royal Oak Foundation Showhouse, New York, New York; pages 92 and 93, the Pasadena Showhouse, Pasadena, California; page 96, the Royal Oak Foundation Showhouse, New York, New York; page 100, the Atlanta Symphony Associates Decorators Showhouse, Atlanta, Georgia; page 101, the Mansions and Millionaires Showhouse, Sands Point, New York; pages 102-105, the Litchfield County Designer Showhouse, Roxbury, Connecticut; pages 110-111, the Mansions in May Showhouse, Morristown, New Jersey; page 117, the French Designers Showhouse, New York, New York; pages 118-119, the Junior League of Boston Decorators' Showhouse, Boston, Massachusetts; pages 122-125, the Junior League of Hartford Showhouse, Hartford, Connecticut; pages 128-29, the Locust Valley Showhouse, Locust Valley, New York; page 130, the Junior League of Boston 25th Anniversary Decorator Show House, Boston, Massachusetts.